A Woman for All Seasons

Meditations for All Seasons

Margaret Anna Cusack
"The Nun of Kenmare"

Copyright © 2015 Dominic G. Ciriaco

All rights reserved. No part of this book may be reproduced or transmitted in any form or by any means, electronic or mechanical, including photocopying, recording, or by any information storage or retrieval system now existing or to be invented, without written permission from the respective copyright holder(s), except for the inclusion of brief quotations in a review.

The Scripture citations used in this work are taken from *The New American Bible*, copyright © 2000-2001 by Fireside Bible Publishers, Wichita, KS.

Painting of Margaret Anna Cusack on the back cover by Gerald Hubert. Photo of Our Lady of Knock from the author's private collection. All other images are from the archives of the sisters of St. Joseph of Peace, Englewood Cliffs, NJ. Used with permission.

Published by Leonine Publishers LLC
Phoenix, Arizona
USA

ISBN-13: 978-1-942190-16-5
Library of Congress Control Number: 2015947548

Printed in the United States of America
10 9 8 7 6 5 4 3 2 1

Visit us online at www.leoninepublishers.com
For more information: info@leoninepublishers.com

A Woman for All Seasons

Meditations for All Seasons

Margaret Anna Cusack
"The Nun of Kenmare"

Compiled, Edited, and Commented
by

Rev. Dominic G. Ciriaco

Leonine Publishers
Phoenix, AZ

Margaret Anna Cusack
(1829-1899)

Contents

Foreword vii

Introduction 1

The Sundays of Advent 27

Christmas Day, Christmas Week, and Epiphany 51

The Five Sundays of Lent and Holy Week 85

Easter Sunday, Easter Week, and Trinity Sunday 151

The Blessed Virgin Mary 183

Various Saints 199

Sayings of Margaret Anna Cusack to Reflect Upon 213

Sources 225

Foreword

I grew up in Jersey City, and was involved in church activities throughout my life—yet I had never known the name of Margaret Anna Cusack, the founder of the Congregation of the Sisters of Saint Joseph of Peace. Consequently, I was surprised to learn, through the following manuscript, that in fact she had been stationed in Jersey City at one point in her ministry; and that the work of her community continues there in three places: at St. Anne's Home, St. Joseph's School for the Blind, and the Cusack Care Center. I am grateful to Father Dominic Ciriaco for making me aware of the life, ministry, and teaching of this remarkable woman.

As Father Ciriaco has demonstrated, Margaret Anna Cusack's life is an illustration of the tension that can exist between the prophet and the established organization. Ciriaco situates Margaret Anna's passions for the poor, and for the proper role of women in society, within the context of other remarkable women who labored in England, Ireland, and the United States during the late 19th and early 20th centuries.

Perhaps because I am a bishop myself, I find Margaret's conflict with the hierarchy to be especially saddening. It challenges all of us to remember that we need to truly collaborate with one another by recognizing the unique gifts that each of us has. As Ciriaco shows, her ministry anticipated many of the values that were promoted by the Second Vatican Council.

I highly recommend to the reader the spiritual and liturgical reflections of Margaret Anna Cusack herself. They illustrate beyond question that she had deep insight into the meaning of the Gospels—and that she was inspired to live those values in a dramatic way. To meditate on these insights, and the benefit that we gain by following her example, is a continuation of her mission for us all.

Bishop John W. Flesey
Auxiliary Bishop of Newark
March 19, 2014
Feast of St. Joseph

Introduction

I first learned about Margaret Anna Cusack when I was in seminary. Some of the seminarians, who were a year ahead of me, were doing summer field work at a hospital in New Jersey which was run by Margaret Anna Cusack's congregation of religious sisters, the Sisters of Saint Joseph of Peace. I recall thinking that the seminarians' opinions of the sisters were not very favorable; they thought the sisters were a little too "liberal" for their tastes. I remember being then told that the foundress of the order must have been a radical and a liberal, because she left the Church towards the end of her life. I laughed to myself as I heard them say, "That's where they must get their liberal thinking from." All of this must have left an impression on me, because I thought to myself, "How can a nun, who is the founder of a religious order, leave the Church?" I jumped to the conclusion that she must have left in response to theological issues. I then dismissed her completely, without even knowing her story. The fact that she had left the Church was enough for me to mark her as a dissenter.

Years later, I discovered a book about Margaret Anna Cusack, entitled *Peace Pays a Price* by Dorothy Vidulich. This book opened my eyes to the story and message of Margaret Anna Cusack, the Nun of Kenmare. I learned that the reasons why she left the Church were not theological. Instead, it was because she spoke out against injustices taking place in the Church and society, and defended the poor. She would become a marked woman, being a threat to certain members of the Church of her time. I realized that I had dismissed her for the same reasons that so many had during her lifetime. By not understanding who she was or what she stood for, I judged her without knowing her; a problem we tend to get caught up in today as members of our church and society.

As I began to read more about Margaret Anna Cusack, I began to fall in love with her and with her message. I no longer saw her as a threat to my understanding of the Church, but as both a challenge and a help for me to understand people within the Church. The more I read of her writings and her books, the more I saw what a genius she was. She was truly a prophet in her time—and she was persecuted for what she believed. She embodied the ideals of the Second Vatican Council, which would not take place until almost one hundred years later. I am convinced that her story must be shared with the Church at large; not just with her religious community of sisters and associates, but with the faithful of today, especially with bishops and priests.

What happened to her then should not happen now. Sadly enough it still does, on many levels. Margaret Anna Cusack remained unknown from the time of her death in 1899 until the 1960s, when the Second Vatican Council asked religious orders to re-discover the message and charism of their founders and foundresses. Even Margaret Anna Cusack's own religious congregation seems to have erased her from its memory, as though it were ashamed because she left the Church and was silenced by the hierarchy of her day.

All that changed with the Second Vatican Council. Margaret Anna Cusack was re-discovered and appreciated for her message of peace and justice. Slowly, could we in the Church begin to recognize this message of hers and use it as an example of how we can dialogue more with people who challenge the Church? Margaret Anna's example can help others understand the Church's position and vice versa. This is why I have come to appreciate Margaret Anna's example, because it is timeless. She still challenges us to reach out to the poor and to speak out on issues of peace and justice. I have also come to realize that her message would be more powerful and effective if she had remained in the Church.

Saint Thomas More, that great English statesman and martyr for the Faith, is known as "A Man for All Seasons." He is called this because he was very successful in many different roles: Christian, lawyer, husband, father, writer, Lord Chancellor of England. He has inspired so many people over the centuries. And if Saint Thomas More is a "man for all seasons" then Margaret Anna Cusack is a "woman for all seasons." She was successful in the many different roles and responsibilities she had: as a religious sister, a writer, an activist, a foundress, and a faithful Christian. She also has inspired many. That is why I am calling this book *A Woman for All Seasons*. The title also alludes to her collection of meditations for the liturgical year which are gathered here.

The powerful voice and example of Margaret Anna Cusack are rooted in the era that she lived in, as are the other religious and political figures of her time who enabled her to leave her mark on the Church and on nineteenth-century society. Her life spans seventy years of that century, as it emerged from the Victorian era. The strength and leadership abilities of Queen Victoria would greatly influence Margaret Anna Cusack. This was also the era of the Industrial Revolution, which saw great advancements in technology through the production of factories and machines. However, poor working conditions and exploitation of workers would become dominant problems, and were issues which Margaret Anna spoke out against. These conditions have been explored in famous literary works such as *Oliver Twist* and *A Christmas Carol* by Charles Dickens. I am sure that, being literate, Margaret Anna must have read these classics, which would have opened her eyes to the plight of workers and the poor. She experienced firsthand the Irish Potato Famine that brought about such poverty-stricken conditions in Ireland. She wrote extensively to politicians and land owners, seeking to help the poor and to create a just system for them.

Florence Nightingale was a contemporary of Margaret Anna Cusack. They knew one another and Margaret Anna admired Florence, who trained nurses during the Crimean War and created better sanitation conditions for the wounded soldiers. Margaret Anna was part of an Anglican sisterhood that also took up this work.

The Women's Rights Movement began to build strength during the nineteenth century. Both Susan B. Anthony and Elizabeth Cady Stanton were contemporaries of Margaret Anna Cusack. All three began to write and to speak out on women's issues during a time when women were treated as second-class citizens.

During the nineteenth century the two popes that would greatly influence Margaret Anna Cusack would be Pius IX and Leo XIII. There was mutual respect between Margaret Anna and both of these popes, and they provided encouragement for her as she worked towards peace and justice. Pope Pius IX encouraged Margaret Anna to write books and even praised her biography on Saint Patrick. Pope Leo XIII encouraged the establishment of her congregation of the Sisters of Peace of Saint Joseph. He praised her work on behalf of the poor, and provided her with a letter of support to be presented to any diocese she went to as she collected funds for those in need. Sadly, many ecclesiastics in the United States rejected her, even with this papal blessing. Even with papal approval, she was faced with resistance!

Another great influence on Margaret Anna Cusack would have been the Oxford Movement. There was a period in English history when many Anglicans returned to the Roman Catholic Church, rediscovering their roots as emphasized in the Early Church. Blessed John Henry Newman, a great leader in the Oxford Movement, was a contemporary of Margaret Anna, and no doubt an encouragement to her. Cardinal Wiseman, another leader of the Oxford Movement, would also have been an inspiration to Margaret Anna, for he received her into the Catholic Church.

As a Woman for All Seasons, Margaret Anna Cusack spoke out on behalf of the poor and the less fortunate. She believed in the dignity of the human person, and knew that education should be accessible to all. Peace and justice were the hallmarks of her religious congregation of women.

Margaret Anna crossed paths with many other influential men and women in the Church who promoted the same work and ideals as she. In Ireland, during the late eighteenth and early nineteenth centuries, Venerable Catherine McAuley established social institutions to aid the poor, as well as founded the Sisters of Mercy. At one point, Margaret Anne was encouraged by Cardinal Wiseman to join these sisters, though she would eventually be led to join the Poor Clare Nuns. Venerable Nano Nagle was another influential figure, on whose work of social reform Margaret Anna would model her own. Nano Nagle founded the Sisters of the Presentation of Mary, who were pioneers in education.

During her years in England, Margaret Anna would have crossed paths with Genevieve Dupuis, who founded the Sisters of Charity of Saint Paul the Apostle. This was an English order of women who performed great works of charity, and it would be these sisters who would minister to Margaret Anna during the final days of her illness. Even though she was no longer a Roman Catholic, these Catholic sisters gave Margaret Anna spiritual encouragement on her deathbed.

Elizabeth Prout was another influential English woman who ministered to the poor and neglected during Margaret Anna's lifetime. Elizabeth Prout founded a congregation of Religious Sisters known as the Sisters of the Cross and Passion.

Venerable Mary Potter, from Nottingham, England, founded the Little Company of Mary, a religious order of women dedicated to hospital work. Her congregation took their vows in Saint Barnabas Cathedral in Nottingham, England, around the same time that Margaret Anna Cusack and her first followers took their vows.

It was Bishop Bagshawe of Nottingham who helped to establish both these congregations; he worked with Mary Potter at one point, and later on with Margaret Anna Cusack.

When Mother Cusack crossed the Atlantic to come to the United States, she worked in New York and New Jersey at the same time that Saint Francis Xavier Cabrini was there, helping the poor and the immigrants. Mother Cabrini aided the Italian immigrants while Mother Cusack reached out to the Irish immigrants.

If Margaret Anna Cusack were alive today I am sure she would be a supporter of social reform, speaking out for the poor and marginalized. Perhaps she would lead a peace and justice march, or participate in a peaceful rally to end a war, or campaign against immigration laws in order to aid illegal aliens. She might well be tweeting and she already has a Facebook page. Social media would have been used to her advantage, since she wrote so much during the nineteenth century. Today she would reach a much wider and more diverse audience. I have no doubt that Pope Francis, like his predecessor Pope Leo XIII, would bless her work and encourage her. However, this time, people would listen to her message—and she would receive the respect that she deserved but did not encounter in her own time. As we now know, Margaret Anna Cusack *is* a Woman for All Seasons. She appeals to so many and has accomplished so much. Her message is as relevant to us today as it was one hundred years ago.

I have come a long way since my seminary days, and since my first encounter with Margaret Anna Cusack. She has taught me a lot about the plight of the poor and the need to respect all people, and especially how to be respectful and willing to listen to others. She has taught me about the Church, how it operates, and how other peoples' influences can make or break a person. She has taught me about prayer and about how the liturgical seasons help us to enter into the mystery of Christ's suffering, death, and rising. Most importantly, she has taught me about Christ, and how to see Him in everyday events, persons, and seasons.

Ultimately, this book is a Margaret Anna Cusack Reader. It combines my reflections on her life with a collection of her own reflections, to help you pray throughout the liturgical seasons. She wrote these reflections for the liturgical year when she was the Nun of Kenmare. Here, you will come in contact with the soul of Margaret Anna Cusack, as she leads you closer to Christ.

My hope for you, as you read this book about Margaret Anna Cusack and reflect upon her writings, is that you will grow closer to Christ. I pray that Margaret Anna Cusack, a Woman for All Seasons, may become for you an example of true discipleship in Jesus Christ.

Who Is Margaret Anna Cusack, The Nun of Kenmare?

THE ANGLICAN YEARS

Margaret Anna Cusack was born on May 6th, 1829, in Dublin, Ireland. Her mother was Sara Stoney Cusack and her father was Dr. Samuel Cusack. Her ancestry was rooted in Anglo-Irish aristocracy. Although she was raised in comfortable surroundings, she did not grow up in a wealthy atmosphere. Her family members were strict Anglicans and they adhered to that church's teachings and beliefs. In her autobiography, *The Story of My Life*, Margaret Anna remembers that from a very young age she was brought to church on Sundays on a regular basis. She writes: "I used to delight in the Sunday School class, when I was old enough to understand its meaning, and we were not sent to this until we could understand" (Cusack 18).

From a very young age she learned to love her faith and was given an example of love and service to the poor by her father. He was a medical doctor who gave up a lucrative medical practice to give service to the poor. During an epidemic of cholera, her father became very sick. Eventually it would lead to his premature death and the breakup of the family. Dr. Cusack's widow and his children then moved to Exeter, England, to live with Margaret Anna's grandmother. It was here that she was encouraged to study, read, and write. She became an avid reader, which gave her an opportunity that most girls of the nineteenth century were not granted. She writes in her autobiography: "My education was principally carried on at home. My dear Grannie had high ideas of education, and fortunately for me I was a willing scholar, and only too glad to take advantage of all the opportunities which she offered me" (Cusack 29). Her love for her faith was also further encouraged by her grandmother.

Finding Love, and the Death of Her Fiancé

"I now come to a part of my life's history which would thankfully pass by in silence, but I feel it would be an injustice to the reader if I did so, since the consequences of what I have to record so completely changed the whole course of my life" (Cusack 47). In this sentence, Margaret Ana is referring to her one and only true love, Charles Holmes, and the sad events that surrounded her relationship with him. During her younger years she had many friends, and Charles Holmes was a close friend whose friendship turned to romance as the years went by. His father was an erudite Anglican minister. Both Charles and Margaret Ann shared the same passion for study and the same views on life. She felt that she had found her soul mate, and they planned to marry. While on a trip to Ireland to visit some family, Margaret Anna's fiancé Charles died unexpectedly of a sudden illness.

Margaret Anna's world was turned upside down. Now both of the men whom she loved dearly, her father and fiancé, were gone.

"I lay in a darkened room for months, for it seemed to me as if even the sunlight was too glad. I scarcely spoke, and I wept until it was a marvel that the fountain of my tears was not dried up forever" (Cusack 32). This was a life changing event for Margaret Anna Cusack; one that left her in despair and caused her soul to search for two years, seeking what she should do next. Her answer came in meeting Dr. Edward Pusey, a leader in the Oxford Movement, who was trying to bring about unity between the Anglican church and the Catholic Church without leaving the former. Unlike John Henry Newman, another leader in the Oxford Movement, who broke away from the Anglican church completely and joined the Roman Catholic Church, Dr. Pusey remained an Anglican. Margaret Anna was greatly influenced by him and his preaching. It led her to decide to become an Anglican sister. Over a period of time, however, she became disillusioned with what she saw in the Anglican convent and with Dr. Pusey himself. Margaret Anna began to see that the women in the Anglican convent were not leading authentic lives and that Dr. Pusey seemed to be controlling the way they lived. More soul-searching helped her to realize that "[she] did not believe in offering the gospel of talk to starving people." She believed that the gospels should be put into action. This led her to further explore the Roman Catholic Church.

Catholic Conversion

Through the Oxford Movement, Margaret Anna Cusack found her way into the Catholic Church. In her book, *The Nun of Kenmare*, she recalls: "I was received into the Roman Catholic Church on the Second of July 1858. The change of opinion which led me from the Anglican into the Roman Catholic Church occurred at a period when I was suffering from a long illness" (Cusack 11). She states that during this period, she began to read the writings of prominent Catholic converts such as Manning and Newman; through this reading she began to grasp the idea of a visible church, as she longed for certainty in faith.

It was the famous Cardinal Wisemen who received Margaret Anna into the Church and confirmed her. At this point she knew that she wanted to give her life to the service of the Church by entering a convent, but she did not know which one to consider, and was advised to wait a while. Cardinal Wisemen gave her two suggestions at this time: first, to consider joining the Sisters of Mercy and second, to take up her pen and write.

Writing Some Hundred Volumes

Not only is Margaret Anna Cusack a religious figure; she is a literary figure as well. She became known as the "Nun of Kenmare" through the many books she wrote as a Poor Clare nun in her monastery in Kenmare, Ireland. She reached thousands of people through her writings which were published not only in her native Ireland but throughout the world. Her works were translated into French, German, and Spanish, and the subjects ranged from religion to politics. She published spiritual works, biographies of saints and political figures, and studies on Irish history. A Life of the Blessed Virgin Mary, biographies on Saints Columba, Brigid, and Patrick, and on Pius IX, were some of her spiritual works. Pope Pius IX praised her books, especially her biography on Saint Patrick.

Her political pieces and commentaries on society included *Woman's Work in Modern Society*, *Woman's Place in the Economy of Creation*, *The Famine in Ireland*, and *The Life and Times and Writings of Daniel O'Connell, the Liberator of Ireland*. Many of these books brought her negative criticism.

Later in life she wrote two autobiographies: *The Nun of Kenmare* and *The Story of My Life*. Despite negative criticism, the money generated from her books supported the Poor Clare community and their work with the poor. While her books may have been controversial to some, they were inspiring to many others. Many of her books have been reprinted today, offering the possibility of inspiration to a whole new generation.

Her Years with the Poor Clares

Upon her conversion to the Catholic Church, Margaret Anna Cusack felt drawn to enter the religious life. She chose not to enter the Sisters of Mercy or the Dominicans, and instead settled on the Poor Clare Sisters of Newry, in County Down. She entered on July 2nd, 1859. She was drawn to the lives of Saint Francis of Assisi and Saint Clare and their commitment to poverty. These two great saints lived an authentic way of life based on the gospels. During their time in the twelfth century, it drew many followers to do the same. Margaret Anna Cusack was drawn to this in the nineteenth century. It is what was lacking in her Anglican sisterhood. Franciscan spirituality would open her heart to recognize the plight of the poor, and to take action to help them.

During her time as a Poor Clare, Margaret Anna Cusack's literary works flourished. She became known at this time as the "Nun of Kenmare." All proceeds from her books went towards helping the poor and her religious community. She began to become more vocal on behalf of the impoverished, challenging both institutions and people of influence. Of course, this is what would eventually get her in trouble, as some political and church leaders would feel threatened by her work.

In 1879, she founded the Famine Relief Fund. Margaret Anna explains the purpose of this fund in her first autobiography:

> The object of my fund was, first, to supplement, as far as possible the relief, often wholly inadequate, given by the public funds. Second, to enable clergymen of all denominations, and sisters, to exercise a most necessary discretion in assisting their destitute people, and to enable them to give such help in cases of severe sickness or weakness, as would not be allowed to be given from the public funds (Cusack 91).

This fund provided assistance for many people who were in dire need. As stated before, her defense of the poor got her into trouble as she spoke out strongly and more often, criticizing landowners, especially, who were evicting tenants without good reason. Court cases ensued and the Nun of Kenmare had to testify on behalf of others. These cases were well publicized by the media of the time. The Nun of Kenmare received letters from supporters as well as critics of her testimony.

In addition to this, Margaret Anna began to criticize the wealth of the Church's hierarchy. Her infamy began to grow.

Founding a New Community

Many of the influences and struggles that Margaret Anna Cusack experienced as a Poor Clare nun would direct her to establish a religious community of her own. There were also several personal experiences that would set the stage for the Sisters of Saint Joseph of Peace to come into existence. Her direct work with the poor would lay the foundation for a community of women who could reach out to those who were most in need. As a Poor Clare nun, she was cloistered. She could not leave the monastery, so she performed all of her social justice work from within its cloistered walls. Her influence as a cloistered nun was impressive.

When she founded a new order, she decided that her community would not be cloistered but would go out among the people, assisting them. The struggles she endured for being outspoken proved to her the need for a religious order of women who would promote peace. In the Constitutions of the Congregation that were written in 1884 it states: "...to promote the peace of the church both by word and work. The very name Sisters of Peace will, it is hoped, inspire the desire of peace and a love for it."

The events she would experience in Knock, Ireland, would also put into play the establishment of the Sisters of Saint Joseph of Peace. Margaret Anna Cusack traveled to Knock on November 18th, 1881, for a two-fold reason. First, she was in poor health, and she sought some spiritual consolation at the Shrine of Our Lady of Knock, where it was reported that the Blessed Virgin Mary had appeared. (Margaret Anna Cusack did report that she experienced a cure at the Knock Shrine, for afterwards her health began to improve.) Her second reason for coming to Knock was to establish a Poor Clare convent and school for girls, which she did accomplish. This experience would lead her to establish a community of women who would help poverty-stricken girls improve their living situations through education.

The Knock school inspired young women to discern their vocation to the religious life. One such woman was Honoria Gaffney. When she met Margaret Anna Cusack, a friendship was forged between the two women. Honoria Gaffney would later become Mother Evangelista, and she would help establish the Sisters of Saint Joseph of Peace. It was at this time of the new congregation's founding that Margaret Anna Cusack becomes not only the foundress but the head of the community and is now referred to as Mother Cusack. Mother Cusack's work with the poor, coupled with her outspokenness, would be met with opposition by the hierarchy of the church and the local bishop would eventually ask Mother Cusack to leave his diocese.

The local bishop became upset with Mother Cusack because her work with the poor crossed lines with the local politicians. Cusack became very critical of the politicians who did not help the poor. She also became critical of the hierarchy who, as she would state, lived well-off among the less fortunate. This led her to leave the diocese. What one has to understand here is that it was not proper for a woman during the Victorian Era to first speak out this way; and second, improper to do so towards men in these different areas of politics and religion. This reputation is what follows her to America where it will haunt her later.

When Margaret Anna Cusack left the Poor Clares to establish a new congregation of women, she was received with open arms by Bishop Edward Gilpin Bagshawe of Nottingham, England. The Sisters of Saint Joseph of Peace were founded on January 7th, 1884, when Margaret Anna Cusack, Honoria Gaffney, and four other women made their profession of vows before Bishop Bagshawe in the Lady Chapel of Saint Barnabas Cathedral in Nottingham. Their first mission was established in England at Great Grimsby on January 9th, 1884. Thus began their work of peace and justice, and this work continued to develop and expand. Mother Cusack and Mother Evangelista would travel to Rome to receive Papal Approval for the new congregation. They attended a private audience with Pope Leo XIII on May 18th,

1884. The Pope gave authorization and blessed the new community of the Sisters of Peace, encouraging Mother Cusack to continue her work for the poor.

She left Rome in June of 1884 with a light heart and no doubts in her mind. She did not foresee that her work would be met with opposition, and could not possibly have anticipated what would happen next.

Attempts to Work in the United States

Margaret Anna Cusack returned to Nottingham with great joy. Not only had her congregation been approved by the Vatican, but Pope Leo XIII had blessed her work and given her a letter of introduction to be used wherever she travelled. She was dispensed from her vows as a Poor Clare nun and could now wholeheartedly embrace her new life as a Saint Joseph Sister of Peace.

Bishop Bagshawe had encouraged Margaret Anna and the other sisters to open missions throughout England and attend to the needs of the poor. Schools were opened to educate young girls and empower them to learn a trade and develop leadership skills. Margaret Anna looked extensively for work for the Sisters of Saint Joseph of Peace, but it was challenging in the area in which they lived. Bishop Bagshawe again encouraged Margaret Anna to look towards the United States, and venture there to collect funds for the poor. Many Irish had already immigrated to the United States and were in need of assistance themselves. With Mother Evangelista Gaffney and a chaplain as her companions, Margaret Anna Cusack set sail for New York on October 24th, 1884. Upon their arrival in New York they were supposed to be received by Cardinal John McCloskey, but he had fallen ill. His assistant, Archbishop Michael Corrigan, would not be able to receive them for three years. Ultimately Archbishop Corrigan would not receive her at all into the Archdiocese of New York due to the negative reputation she earned as the Nun of

Kenmare in Ireland. This negative reputation stemmed from some of her writings that were met with opposition by some. Her criticizing the Irish politicians and Catholic hierarchy in the treatment of the poor became her downfall.

Across the river, however, in the Diocese of Newark, New Jersey Bishop Winand Wigger would accept her, and praise her work with the poor. In working with the poor, Mother Cusack educated them and raised a substantial amount of money from the publishing of her books. This was used to feed the poor and provide clothing and shelter for them. She was able to open a convent in Jersey City. She was also able to purchase property and to open a home for working women as well as an orphanage for children. More sisters were sent from England to Jersey City, and the congregation began to spread in the United States. Property was then purchased in Englewood Cliffs, New Jersey, so that another convent and a facility for working women could be established. With her congregation beginning to flourish, Margaret Anna Cusack was now ready to tour the different dioceses to collect funds for her projects and for the poor.

Stepping Aside So That Her Congregation Can Flourish

It was Margaret Anna Cusack's desire to open a school for the blind. Bishop Wigger of Newark granted her permission to do so. He also suggested that she travel to other dioceses to collect funds to help with the new establishment, and he granted her two months permission to leave her convent in order to travel and raise the funds. From Philadelphia to Baltimore to Washington D.C., Margaret Anna met with many bishops, and asked for their assistance. Many rejected her requests, as they did not see the need to establish such schools at that time. It was Cardinal Gibbons of Baltimore who recognized the need for Margaret Anna's work. He knew that the Catholic University of America in Washington, D.C., was under construction, and that dioceses were being asked to fund and support this project. He knew that Margaret Anna's fund would compete with this. He was also aware that Margaret Anna Cusack's negative reputation had caught up with her and that this would cause many dioceses from helping her cause.

Archbishop Corrigan of New York spread the word among other prelates to be wary of the "Nun of Kenmare." At this point, with dioceses not welcoming her in, doors would shut on Margaret Anna and her project.

This brought great distress to Margaret Anna, for she saw that the work and spirit of the Saint Joseph Sisters of Peace could not grow or be appreciated. Margaret Anna criticized Archbishop Corrigan and several other priests in the diocese over their lack of support for the poor. This can be said to have been the final nail hammered into the coffin of Margaret Anna's work. It would prevent her and her community from being actively involved in future opportunities. Bishop Wigger of Newark supported Archbishop Corrigan of New York who was criticized by Mother Cusack again about her perception of his negligence with issues with the poor and land rights for them. Although Bishop Wigger at first supported her work, he now pulled away from her, withdrawing his support.

At this point, Margaret Anna Cusack knew that as long as her name was associated with the Saint Joseph Sisters of Peace, the congregation would cease to exist. Further discernment led her to make a painful decision: she decided to disassociate from the congregation, as well as leave the order and the Roman Catholic Church. She had been pushed around too much by the hierarchy for her to see any value in staying and continuing her work for the poor. This has to be her most courageous and selfless act of humility: stepping aside so that the good work for the poor that the sisters had been performing could continue to grow. She knew that peace and justice must continue in this fashion.

Still, not since the death of her fiancé had she experienced such pain, loneliness, and distress. In her second autobiography, *The Story of My Life*, she records this painful memory:

> At last the day came on which I was to bid farewell for ever to sisters who, whatever may have been their quarrels with each other, were certainly most true and faithful to their Mother. Those who think it a light matter to leave all things for conscience sake know little indeed of what it cost me at my age, and in my peculiar circumstances, to obey the call of God. I went out literally not knowing whither I went, and knowing nothing of protestant fear of and subjection to Rome in America (p. 386).

Her Return to Anglicanism

Margaret Anna Cusack was fifty-nine years old when she left her community and the Catholic Church. The majority of her family had passed away and she was not at an age to start a new career. Where would she turn? Who would help her now? Margaret Anna went back to the familiarity of her childhood and returned to the Anglican church. She became good friends with an Episcopalian bishop, Frederick Dan Huntington, of Massachusetts. Bishop Huntington himself was a great defender of the poor and spoke out on social justice issues. His son, James Otis Sergeant Huntington, was the founder of the Anglo-Catholic Benedictine Community of the Holy Cross. (He is honored as a saint in the Episcopal Church today.) Bishop Huntington and his wife invited Margaret Anna to come live with them in Massachusetts. She was grateful for their kindness and support at a very low point in her life, and she accepted their offer.

Eventually, Margaret Anna would live by herself in Massachusetts. For the last ten years of her life she would go on speaking tours, and continue to write books on her experience as a Catholic nun. The proceeds of her lectures and books would support her. It is possible to catch glimpses of what she endured at this time through this passage in *The Story of My Life*: "My advanced age and very delicate health made it doubly trying for me to leave the only home I had. My near relatives were all dead, and I was alone in the world, and had to trust entirely to strangers. How cruelly my trust was betrayed. I have never told, but I tell it now for the help of others" (Cusack 384-385). After a few years of touring the United States and giving lectures, Margaret Anna Cusack decided to return to England, and to there spend her final years on this earth.

Illness and Final Years

Margaret Anna Cusack was right. When she disassociated herself from the Saint Joseph Sisters of Peace, doors of opportunity opened up for the congregation, and it spread, taking up apostolic works in others dioceses in the United States. The sisters were invited to Tacoma, Washington, where a hospital and convent were built. Mother Evangelista Gaffney, close confidant and friend of Margaret Anna, took over the helm of the congregation, and at this time became known as its foundress. Mother Evangelista Gaffney was the first follower of Margaret Anna Cusack's vision for a new congregation of sisters and she became its first member. She was a confidant to Mother Cusack, stood by her and defended her actions when Cusack was going through her trials. Mother Evangelista continued to correspond with Cusack after she left the community and the Church. It was only appropriate then to make Mother Evangelista not only the head of the congregation but to consider her a foundress. She would continue the vision and ideas of Cusack. The student now becomes the teacher.

They altered the name of the congregation to the Sisters of Saint Joseph of Newark, since the motherhouse was now located in the Diocese of Newark, New Jersey. Slowly the influence of Margaret Anna Cusack began to disappear. When she returned to England, she would again take up her pen and write. Most notably she wrote another autobiography entitled *The Story of My Life*. She also wrote a history of the Jesuit Order entitled *The Black Pope*, as well as another book about her experiences in the Roman Catholic Church entitled *What Rome Teaches*. She kept in contact through letters with Mother Evangelista, but was never allowed to see her dear sisters again.

Margaret Anna's poor health, which had plagued her her whole life, would now begin to deteriorate even more. But in her last months and days on this earth, she had the support and care of many friends who embraced her as she returned to England. On her deathbed she was ministered to by a Reverend Gregory from the local Anglican church in Exeter. The Catholic Sisters of Charity of Saint Paul came to visit with her, and kept the Sisters of Saint Joseph informed of her condition. Margaret Anna Cusack died with the blessing of the Anglican church on June 5th, 1899. She was seventy years old.

An Ecumenical Example

Margaret Anna Cusack died surrounded by friends from the Anglican community, Catholic sisters from her own congregation, and the Sisters of Charity of Saint Paul, united in prayer. This gives her death, and her life for that matter, an ecumenical dimension. She began life as an Anglican, became Catholic, but returned to the Anglican fold at the end of her life. She reminds us that today we should be in ecumenical dialogue with our sisters and brothers from other Christian traditions and other faith traditions.

Ecumenism is a call from the Second Vatican Council for Catholics to reach out in dialogue. Margaret Anna Cusack's life models this for us as Protestants were willing to visit her on her deathbed. She reminds us that Christ's call to reach out to the less fortunate, and to put His teachings into practice, is a call for all Christians. She reminds us that we should listen to each other, not to judge, but to enter into dialogue, especially when we are feeling challenged. I cannot help but think that if the bishops of her time had done this, she would have stayed in the Catholic Church, and they could have worked through the issues she raised during her lifetime. The "threat" that Margaret Anna Cusack was to the hierarchy of her day is quite trivial today. Today it is possible to see her as a prophet. She embraced the ideas of the Second Vatican Council decades before they were ever discussed and implemented.

Lessons From Margaret Anna Cusack's Life

At times the lives of holy people are to be admired but not imitated. On certain levels this is true about Margaret Anna Cusack. While her charitable work is to be both admired and imitated, her exodus from the Catholic Church in the final years of her life is challenging to comprehend, and of course, as people of faith, not to be imitated. Obviously, Margaret Anna Cusack had her reason to do something so drastic as abandon the beauty of the Catholic faith. I often wonder if she lived today or if there were different circumstances to her situation, would she have stayed?

St. Mary MacKillop, Australia's first saint, encountered similar circumstances as Margaret Anna Cusack; they both came into conflict with their local bishops. St. Mary MacKillop was even temporarily excommunicated by her bishop because they disagreed. This was a painful time for St. Mary MacKillop, and she accepted it and endured with the strength of her faith. She did not despair but found hope in her faith. Eventually Blessed Pope Pius IX lifted the excommunication ban imposed upon her and was received back into the Church.

Margaret Anna Cusack also was in conflict with her local bishop but it seems that Margaret Anna was too stubborn to step back, process it all in, and humbly take the higher ground to at least "agree to disagree" and move on. For Margaret Anna Cusack, her social justice work and the religious congregation of sisters were at stake. Unlike St. Mary MacKillop, Mother Cusack saw no hope in her situation. She sacrificed leaving the Catholic faith in order for her religious congregation of the Sisters of St. Joseph of Peace to flourish and grow and so her charitable establishments could continue.

In his book *Faithful Dissenters: Stories of Men and Women who Loved and Changed the Church*, Robert McClory lists several famous men and women who came into conflict with the human authority of the Church but overcame that conflict and triumphed in their Catholic faith. Such people were Galileo, Mary Ward, St. Catherine of Siena, St. Hildegard of Bingen, Matteo Ricci, St. Thomas Aquinas, and Dominican Theologian Yves Congar. In the introduction to his book, McClory writes,

This book is not meant to encourage dissent as a general practice. Throughout history, Church authority in countless instances has followed a course that was wise and prudent, leading to outcomes that can only be considered providential. As a general rule, I believe, Catholics should give that authority the benefit of the doubt. But the Church is a human as well as divine institution; it is not always and everywhere protected from mistaken judgment, pre-mature decision, or the other errors and foibles to which the exercise of authority on this earth is subject…History says that there's good dissent and there's bad dissent, just as in other contexts there's good cholesterol and there's bad cholesterol, good liturgy and bad liturgy, good administration and bad administration (McClory, p. 4).

I can say the same with this book as well. By presenting the life and works of Margaret Anna Cusack, I am not encouraging her dissent; rather, I wish she would have been at peace with herself and the Church but this did not play out in Church history. What I am presenting here is a unique example of a disciple of Christ who contributed a wealth of good to the Church through her social work, her religious congregation of women, and her many spiritual writings which were praised by Popes, Bishops, and the faithful for several centuries. But at the same time, we also learn from Margaret Anna that our mistakes and disagreements should never lead to abandoning the beauty of our Catholic faith. There is always hope!

Gathered here in this book are the Liturgical Meditations of Margaret Anna Cusack, the Nun of Kenmare. They were written over a period of thirty years, as a recent convert to the Catholic Church on fire with her faith, and as a Poor Clare Nun inspiring her fellow nuns. May these meditations do the same for you, inspire you, and make you on fire for the faith.

LEFT: Lady Chapel in the Cathedral of St. Barnabas Nottingham, England. Here Margaret Anna Cusack and her companions took vows as the Sisters of St. Joseph of Peace.

RIGHT: Mother Cusack, Mother Evangelista Gaffney, Bishop Bagshaw: the founders of the Sisters of St. Joseph of Peace.

Convent of the Poor Clare Sisters in Kenmare, Ireland. Here Margaret Anna Cusack became famous as the "Nun of Kenmare" through her writings and charitable works.

LEFT: Statue of Our Lady of Knock. It was at the shrine in Ireland where Margaret Anna Cusack was cured of an illness.

St. Barnabas Cathedral, Nottingham, England.

Grave of Margaret Anna Cusack near Nottingham, England.

The Sundays of Advent

First Sunday of Advent

First Meditation
The Heart of the Infant Jesus, Our Coming Light

"Behold, the Lord comes and all His saints with Him, and in that day there shall be a great light."
(Antiphon at Lauds)

"And the light of the moon will be like the light of the sun, and the light of the sun will be seven times greater, like the light of seven days,
On the day the Lord binds up the wounds of his people and heals the bruises left by his blows."
(Isaiah 30:26)

First Prelude –

Consider the Heart of the Infant Jesus in the womb of Mary as a flame of clear and beautiful light, coming to enlighten all nations. Consider also the terrible light of the Second Coming, which will be manifested to all.

-Pause and Reflect-

Second Prelude –

Pray that you may be so enlightened by the light of His first coming, that you may not be terrified by the light of the Second Coming.

-Pause and Reflect-

FIRST POINT

Look at the Heart of the Infant Jesus. It lies hidden in the womb of Mary, even as His blessed Humanity will be hidden hereafter in the tabernacle. Oh, what a holy, beautiful, peaceful light is the light of the Infant Heart of Jesus. How it longs to come forth and manifest itself to all, to console, to instruct, to illuminate! Are we, also, longing to receive this Light? Are we praying with our whole hearts that it may come to us, and that we may be prepared to receive it? Great though our spiritual enlightenment may be, we are still, in some measure, "sitting in darkness and in the shadow of death." But the Light is coming; already we can see the dawn upon the mountain. When Mary was born, the first ray of light tinged the eastern sky; when Jesus was born, the light of this mystic moon was as the light of the true sun, because of her perfect union with Him; and the light of the sun was sevenfold, as the light of seven days. The light was sevenfold, that is, the light was perfect, for it was the light of God.

SECOND POINT –

Let us beseech the Infant Jesus to enlighten us in the particular way in which we most need light. We are all born blind through the sin of our first parents, and, unhappily, though we have obtained light in the waters of baptism, we often, by our own fault, lapse into blindness more or less intense. Sometimes we do not wish to see the sin we should forsake, or the virtue we should practice, because it would cost us something to act upon this light. Sometimes we profit so little by the light that it is withdrawn from us, or it is not imported in the fullness and brightness with which more faithful souls are favored. There are souls in whom the light of God shines so brightly that they cannot commit the shadow of an imperfection without perceiving it immediately; there are souls in whom that light shines so resplendently that they see even the shadow of an imperfect motive in the best action they perform. Why should we not be thus favored? It is not because the Light is unwilling to come, but because we are unwilling to receive it.

THIRD POINT –

What shall we do to obtain this great grace? Let us go to Mary. Let us offer our Advent to Mary. Let us consecrate every thought, word, and action to her during this holy season and then, on the blessed morning of Christmas, she will herself place her Infant in our arms; that is, she will lay Him down to rest in our hearts, and He is so obedient to His sweet mother that He will never stir from the heart wherein she places Him, unless she comes to take Him away. Advent should be a time of special devotion to Mary. Jesus again lies mystically in her womb. Again she pleads for us in that blessed Advent when He took flesh of her flesh, and bone of her bone. Oh, let us kneel before her now as we would have knelt before her then, and implore her to intercede for us with Jesus, that He may indeed be our Light, and that we may never be among those who prefer darkness. Then, indeed, may we hope that the Light of His Second Coming will be a light of glory to us, and not a light of condemnation.

ASPIRATION –

Come and enlighten us, O Sweet Infant Jesus.

Form your meditation and place it in the Heart of the Infant Jesus.

Second Meditation
The Heart of the Infant Jesus, Our Coming Purifier

*"Then one of the seraphim flew to me,
holding an ember which he had taken with tongs from the altar. He touched my mouth with it.
'See,' he said, 'Now that this has touched your lips, your wickedness is removed, your sin
purged.'"*

(Isaiah 6:6–7)

FIRST PRELUDE –

Consider the subject of Isaiah's vision: he "saw the Lord sitting upon a throne high and elevated, and his train filled the temple." The Seraphim attend Him, and cry one to the other: "Holy, holy, holy, the Lord God of hosts, all the earth is full of his glory."

SECOND PRELUDE –

Pray that you may be so purified as to adore this God of hosts worthily.

– Pause and Reflect -

FIRST POINT –

Consider the Infant Jesus as our Purifier. He comes that He may touch our lips, not with a live coal from the altar of sacrifice, but with Himself, the Victim of Sacrifice. Even as the Seraphim adored this marvelous vision trembling, and uttering the words Sanctus, Sanctus, Sanctus, which never cease before the Eternal Throne, so did they also tremble and adore, uttering the same canticle of adoration, as they knelt before Mary, when Jesus sat upon the royal throne of her royal womb. And yet we can dare to approach that majesty without fear and without adoration. Advent should be for us a special time of purification. We should purify ourselves to receive our newborn King at Christmas; we should purify ourselves to prepare for the coming of that King, no longer as an Infant and a Purifier, but as a judge and a dispenser of justice. Oh, let us seek to have our lips now so purified by the Sacrifice of the Altar, that they may be worthy of the eternal entrance of our approaching Bridegroom!

SECOND POINT –

Consider the words of this lesson: "They cried one to another, Holy, Holy, and Holy." Thus, also, should we cry to each other, by our words and our example, Holy, Holy, and Holy! Our God is holy, therefore we must be holy. Our God is holy. We are His children; children must be like their father. Our God Who is coming to us is a holy God; He cannot love iniquity, and He will turn away from us if He finds we are not earnest in endeavoring to deliver ourselves from sin—that sin from which He is coming, at such a cost to Himself, to release us. We must give each other good examples: examples of fervor, examples of charity, examples of devotion—crying out one to another, "The Holy One is coming, let us prepare to meet Him."

THIRD POINT –

We need two kinds of purification. When the Seraph touched the lips of the prophet, he said: "Your iniquities shall be taken away, and your sin shall be cleansed." Our Infant Jesus is coming to touch our lips with the kiss of peace, that He may impart to us this twofold purification.

First, He will cleanse all our past sins, that is, He will "take away our iniquities," and we must prepare for this by a good confession, a fervent contrition, and worthy penance. Oh, how earnestly and specially we ought to prepare for our Christmas confession! Jesus is coming to take away our sins; it is but little He asks us to do to obtain so great a grace. And secondly, He will purify us by cleansing us from our daily imperfections and faults. For this we must prepare by commencing now to observe our resolutions with great fidelity, so that our sweet Jesus may find only such imperfections as are inevitable to human frailty.

ASPIRATION –

O my sweet Infant Jesus, touch my lips and my heart, and purify me more and more.

Form your resolutions.

Second Sunday of Advent

FIRST MEDITATION
The Heart of Jesus, the Flower of the Root of Jesse

"But a shoot shall sprout from the stump of Jesse, and from his roots a bud shall blossom. The spirit of the Lord shall rest upon him..."

(Isaiah 11:1–2)

FIRST PRELUDE –

Consider the Infant Jesus as a flower budding in the womb of Mary.

SECOND PRELUDE –

Pray that you may love and cherish this Flower, and that it may be planted in your heart.

- Pause and Reflect -

FIRST POINT –

Consider the words of the prophet: "But a shoot shall sprout from the stump of Jesse, and from his roots a bud shall blossom. The spirit of the Lord shall rest upon him...." Already Mary is recorded in the prophetic page, even as she has already been predestined in the Eternal Counsels as the Mother of Jesus. She is the rod of the root of Jesse, the rod which bears this mystical flower. The stem which supports the flower always corresponds in grace and beauty to the flower which it bears. How beautiful, then, is the stem, Mary, which bears the Flower, Jesus. O Most favored stem! O most holy Flower! The stem nourishes and gives life to the flower. Humanly speaking, the stem is necessary to the flower. Mary nourishes and gives life to Jesus; the sap of this stem, that is the blood of Mary, forms the sacred Humanity of the Flower Jesus. How we should reverence that stem! How we should honor it! How we should strive to protect it from the blasts of dishonor! How we should water it with tears of love and devotion!

Second Point –

The rod, Mary, springs from the root of Jesse. "From this man's descendants God, according to his promise, has brought to Israel a savior, Jesus" (Acts 13:23). Mary springs from a royal and a holy stock, but while the progenitors usually ennoble the scion of a royal house, the scion here ennobles her progenitors. Mary need not glory that she is of the race of David, but David will glory, to all eternity, that Mary sprang from his root. Oh, how deeply this root has entered into the bed of humility, for its branches ascend so high! How great its stability, since it supports God! How marvelous its fertility, since it produces the Author of Creation! Let us bow down in lowly homage before this plant, and adore its Flower, who has called Himself the "Flower of the Field" and the "Lily of the Valley"; the Flower of the fertile field of Mary's virginity, the Lily of the deep valley of her most profound humility.

Third Point –

Let us beware lest we should be "scandalized" at the lowliness of this Flower. Our Lord Himself gives us this warning in today's gospel: "Blessed is he that shall not be scandalized in me." Alas! What fear there should be that we may take scandal at Jesus, when Jesus Himself considered it necessary to pronounce a benediction on those who were not scandalized in Him? We are scandalized in Him when we question the wisdom of His providences and the love of His providences; we are scandalized in Him when we fail to appreciate the greatness of His humility and the beauty of His meekness. The world of heresy is scandalized in Him, because it will not stoop to honor her whom He has stooped so low to exalt. Let us beware lest we should fail, even in the least degree, in the honor due to the stem of Jesse. Let us pray that this Flower may be transplanted into our hearts by her blessed hands, and let us water It with our tears, and cherish It with our love. Then we may hope that the Spirit of the Lord will also rest on us, and fill us with this sevenfold gift.

Second Meditation
The Heart of the Infant Jesus, sending a messenger to prepare His Way

"A voice proclaims: In the wilderness prepare the way of the LORD! Make straight in the wasteland a highway for our God!"

(Isaiah 40:3)

First Prelude –

Consider the great prophet announcing the coming of Jesus.

Second Prelude –

Pray that you may profit by all the messages of grace which Jesus sends you.

First Point –

Consider the exceeding love of Jesus in sending a messenger to prepare His way. When earthly monarchs undertake a journey to a distant part of their dominions, they send messengers before them. These messengers are charged to provide for all their comforts, to remove every obstacle to their advancement, and to warn the people of their approach, that they may conceal all that would prove offensive to royal eyes, banish all semblance of sorrow, and take part in public rejoicings. But our sweet Infant Jesus has no such purpose in sending messengers before His face. Oh, no, His messenger is not charged to see to His comforts; for our coming King, our sweet Infant Jesus, has renounced all comforts. His messenger is not commanded to put out of sight such objects of sorrow and distress as would prove an annoyance to an earthly monarch. No, the messengers of our sweet Jesus were desired to assemble the unhappy and the miserable, to make the most unhappy and the most miserable the most welcome; for our Infant Prince is content to suffer all manner of afflictions Himself, if He can only console one of the poorest of His subjects. He sent us messengers of daily graces, which perhaps we were too much occupied with other things to notice; or if we noticed them, we have forgotten them. Oh, if we only profited by all the messengers Jesus sends us, how different our lives would be!

Second Point –

The voice cries in the desert. Earth is a desert to Jesus, because His Father is not loved and honored there; and yet we try to make a home of the desert, and marvel that we cannot make ourselves comfortable in it. The voice cries in the desert. Jesus is often obliged to make a desert for us, because we will not listen to His voice, or to the voice of His messengers, in the crowded city. When sweet Jesus wants a soul all to Himself, and purposes to do great things in her, He leads her into the very depths of the wilderness. He takes from her all she loves, He makes earth utterly desolate, and He leaves her for a little while to know and feel the bitterness and anguish of His desolation; and then, O then, He Himself comes to her in the wilderness, and the desert rejoices and blossoms like the rose, and the rivers of waters break forth, and the soul, suspended between heaven and earth, lies upon the cross with Jesus, and lives only to love or to suffer, and suffering manifested is here only joy—and love is her reward.

ASPIRATION –

Sweet Infant Jesus, make me faithful to the calls of Your messengers.

Form your resolution!

Third Sunday of Advent

First Meditation
The Heart of the Infant Jesus, Coming to Deliver Us

"The Lord is near. Have no anxiety at all, but in everything, by prayer and petition, with thanksgiving, make your requests known to God."

(Philippians 4:5–6)

First Prelude –

Consider the Infant Jesus in the womb of Mary preparing to come forth and deliver us. Pray that you may profit by all the messages of grace which Jesus sends you.

Second Prelude –

Adore your approaching King with joy and thanksgiving.

- Pause and Reflect -

First Point –

This is the Sunday of Advent joy! The Mass commences with joy: "Rejoice in the Lord always, and again, I say, rejoice." And what is the cause of our joy? "The Lord is nigh!" He is near in the commemorations of His first coming. He is near in the hope of His second coming. He is near, we know not how near, in that swift, sudden coming, which shall be to us the end of time and the commencement of eternity. How many causes, then, we have for joy! When a great prince is born, what rejoicings take place, what great preparations are made even before the birth of a royal child! The nobles prepare gifts, the monarch prepares feasts, and his subjects prepare rejoicings. Shall we not also prepare gifts, and feasts, and rejoicings for our coming Prince? Let each have a gift to offer Him: some daily practice of virtue, some little daily self-denial. And when the day of His birth has come, we can gather our thanksgivings and our devotions into one and lay them at His feet, or, better still, place them in the hands of our Mother to present for us to her Son. The touch of her blessed hand will beautify them, even if her love does not prompt her to add to them from her own treasures.

SECOND POINT –

"Be not solicitous." Why? Because "the Lord is near." What should we think of an heir to a kingdom, who is always fretting about trifles; who, even when his necessities are supplied today, begins to weep because he fears they will not be supplied tomorrow? What should we think of the son of a King, who gives himself up to anxiety about his temporal affairs, because he has some difficulty in managing them in his father's absence, even when he knows that his father is even then coming to deliver him from every embarrassment? O Christian soul, you are the heir of a Kingdom, the child of a King. He is near: why be solicitous? What is there on this earth worth five minutes of anxiety? Or if you must be solicitous, be solicitous for God, and it will not destroy your peace, or hinder your sanctification, as being solicitous for yourself will most assuredly do. Be solicitous for His interests, be solicitous for His Glory, be solicitous to prepare a welcome for Him, and let it be more in prayer and thanksgiving than in restless, busy work.

Third Point –

But if we are commanded to be "nothing solicitous," we are not commanded to be indifferent. We are not told not to work for God in our daily duties, or our spiritual employments; we are not told to have no foresight, or care, or holy thoughtfulness for how our work, spiritual or temporal, may be done best. On the contrary, we must work as if all depended on our labor; we must occupy ourselves earnestly with plans for God's glory and our own sanctification, according to our circumstances and state of life. Still we must not be solicitous—we must not give ourselves up to undue anxiety, to repenting if we fail, to fretting cares. Why? Because "the Lord is coming"—He is coming, He will soon be here, and we shall see that His providence arranged all things, even our contradictions and disappointments, for the best. We must be nothing "solicitous," because we can pray; and if "our requests are made known to God," do we wish that He shall give us what He thinks best, or what we think best? Are we not sure that He hears what we say to Him, and that He will do what He knows is best for us? What reason, then, can we find for being solicitous?

Aspiration –

The Lord is near, O come, let us adore Him.

Form your resolution!

Second Meditation
The Heart of the Infant Jesus, Coming to Enlighten Us Through Mary

"The light of the moon will be like the light of the sun, and the light of the sun will be seven times greater, like the light of seven days, On the day the LORD binds up the wounds of his people and heals the bruises left by his blows."

(Isaiah 30:26)

First Prelude –

Consider the beauty of Mary as she longs with deeper desire each hour to behold her Child and her God.

Second Prelude –

Pray that you may also become spiritually beautiful by your ardent desire for Jesus.

First Point –

Mary, the moon which enlightens the Church, becomes every hour more beautiful. Her light was the one bright spot on a dark earth, when Jesus beheld it from His Father's throne, and came down into her womb. But her light was hidden, for the times of its manifestation had not yet come. Nor will Mary's light be fully manifested until this prophecy has its full accomplishment at the second coming of Jesus. How, indeed, could we bear the fullness of its glory, when even its rays are dazzling to our sinful eyes? But at the moment of the Incarnation the light of the moon did indeed become as the light of the sun. The Sun had concealed Himself in Mary's womb and henceforth she shines with His light. Her light was indeed clear, and new, and beautiful, but now she shines with the light of God, she sees in the light of God, she lives in the light of God.

Second Point –

Hence it is that those who are most devoted to Mary who know Jesus best. They see Him with and in her light, and her light in His. Oh, if we need light to see our imperfections, let us go to Mary, and ask her to show them to us! She sees them in God's light, she sees in what manner they are most offensive to Him. She sees the little specks and motes which we could never discern, because her light "is as the light of the sun," which manifests what is beholden to every light less penetrating. If we need light to discern our path of duty, let us go to Mary. She sees all things in the light of the Sun of Justice for He abides in her. She will shine upon our path in the fullness of heavenly beauty, and if we have the light of Mary's love we shall never lose our road, even when all earthly lights have failed.

Third Point –

The light of the sun fertilizes, and brings the fruits of the earth to perfection, but it also has the power of scorching and destroying. Mary is as a mystical sunlight, fructifying the people of God. Jesus had come "to bind up the wound of His people," and He has made the light of His Mother's love a principal instrument in effecting His blessed end. When the sunshine of Mary's love is turned upon a soul, what graces it obtains, how rapidly it ripens, how marvelously it fructifies, what knowledge it attains! Oh, let us beseech her to look upon us! Her look is life. Once again her Divine Son will come, and then this prophecy will have its perfect accomplishment: "the wound" of God's people will be healed, and the light of Mary will shine with an eternal glory. But there will be another light—a light of fear, a light of destruction. The light of the Sun of Justice will be sevenfold, magnificent to His chosen, destructive to His enemies. Oh, let us pray now that the powerful light of Mary may illuminate and fructify us, lest the destroying light of the last awful day should scorch us for eternity.

ASPIRATION –

Mother of Jesus, be my Mother.

Form your resolution!

Fourth Sunday of Advent

First Meditation

"O Root of Jesse, who stands for an ensign of the people, before Whom Kings are silent, and the nations offer their homage, come and deliver us, and do not delay."
(Antiphon at Magnificat)

"I am the root and stock of David, the bright and morning star."
(Revelation 22:16)

First Prelude –

Consider the Infant Jesus elevating His standard, and inviting all the faithful to place themselves under His protection.

Second Prelude –

Pray that you may march ever faithfully under the standard of this great King.

- Pause and Reflect -

First Point –

The Root of Jesse is still hidden in the mystic earth of Mary's womb, but even now He is preparing to come forth. As the first Adam was made of virgin clay, so is the Second, but woman is now honored in Mary, beyond all that her heart could have hoped and desired. The first woman was formed from man, and hence owed him a debt of gratitude, which she, alas, repaid with evil. The Second Adam is formed of a woman, and from the moment of the Incarnation, the evil which woman had done to man was more than compensated, and man owes a debt of gratitude now to woman. O Mary, who shall tell us how to repay all we owe thee! The mystic ark still contains the hidden manna, but even now He is preparing to come forth and feed His people. O, Mary, what hast thou not given to us!

Second Point –

When Jesus comes forth from the tabernacle, from the Holy of Holies, where He reposes, He will raise His standard, that all nations may assemble beneath it. He invites us with smiles and tears. He assures us that in the war to which He summons us, He will bear the hardest share, and that, however many our defeats, if we only rise up after each and invoke His help, we shall be counted as having won the day. He promises to bear the brunt of the battle, and assures us that He will endure all, and more than all, which the meanest soldier in His camp may suffer, nay, more, He promises that our wounds shall shine resplendent as the sun, and prove no small part of the magnificent adornment He is preparing for us. Who would not desire to enlist under such a leader? Alas, that any should be led astray by the deceitful promises and false protestations of His enemies.

Third Point –

Let us beseech Him to come and deliver us, let us implore Him not to delay, lest our weakness should prove our ruin; let us ask Him to shine upon our souls as the morning star. One day He will come, and angels will display His standard in the heavens. Oh, how many will desire to flock beneath that banner then, who are ashamed to appear even near it now! But it will be too late. That ensign will be a protection to the people of God, but it will be destruction to the enemies of God. That sign of the Cross, which they have despised or viewed with indifference, will be no protection when enemies assail them; but it will be the very mark of the elect, and the token of their being under the protection of the great King.

ASPIRATION –

O sweet Infant Jesus, come and deliver us, and do not delay.

Form your resolution!

SECOND MEDITATION
The Heart of the Infant Jesus, the Key of David

"O Key of David, and scripture of the house of Israel, who open and none can shut, who shuts and none, can open, come and lead us forth from our prison-house, where we sit in darkness and the shadow of death."
(Antiphon at Magnificat)

"Behold I am living forever and ever, and have the keys of death and of Hell."
(Revelation 1:18)

FIRST PRELUDE –

Consider the Infant Jesus coming to offer the keys of the Kingdom of Heaven to the pastors of His Church, that all who desire it may be admitted therein.

Second Prelude –

Pray that the golden key of mercy may open Heaven's doors for you, through the merits of the coming Savior.

-Pause and Reflect-

First Point –

The key is the emblem of power. He who possesses the keys of a palace, is master of the palace. The keys of a city are placed in the hands of its conqueror. Our sweet Jesus comes, as the Key of David, to open to us the royal treasures of that royal house. But we may refuse them; we may imagine the treasures of earth greater and better than the treasures of heaven. Let us not forget that many do deliberately prefer the treasures of earth. Alas! If we should in any measure be so unhappy as to act thus! We prefer earth to heaven when we prefer the pleasures of sin or sense, however trifling, to the boundless treasures which we might obtain by mortification. We occupy our time with what pleases us, instead of with what pleases Jesus. We prefer earth to heaven when we fail in earnestness of purpose, in purity of intention, in attaining that nearness to God to which He is calling us, because we do not like the trouble of constant watchfulness over self.

Second Point –

Consider the power of Him who holds this key. A conqueror may win the keys of a mighty city today, and tomorrow they may be taken from him. A prince may hold the keys of his palace today, and tomorrow the monarch known as death may strike his hand so that he can no longer hold them. But who can snatch the keys from the hand of our Infant Jesus? If He opens the door of the prison house who can close it? If He frees the captive, who can find him again unless he wills to resume his chains? If He opens the golden gate of the palace of David, the "many mansions" of the Father's house, who can close its portals against us? But we must remember, also, that if He shuts none can open. Oh, how we should fear, how we should weep before Him! How we should beseech this gentle Infant that the gates of mercy may never be closed on us! And if we fear that these gates are well-closed because of our sins, let us have recourse to Mary. Jesus has hidden the golden key of mercy in her blessed heart, and she can never refuse to use it for poor sinners; and even if Jesus is obliged to take the key from her, lest she should admit such vile creatures as we are, if we only kneel and weep at her feet, she will kneel at the feet of Jesus, until He gives her the key again, for He can refuse nothing to her, who never refused anything to Him.

THIRD POINT –

But if we desire to obtain all the privileges of the Key of David, if we desire to possess the key of the Sacred Heart of Jesus, we must give Him the key of our hearts. Our sweet Jesus asked Saint Gertrude for the key to her heart, that He might take away from it what He pleased, and place in it what He pleased. But when that saint of love asked Him what this key was, He told her it was her good will! Oh, let us hasten to lay this key at the feet of our Infant Jesus, or rather to place it in His little hands! Let us ask Him to keep it, and never more give it back to us. He will forgive many a fault and many an imperfection to the heart which, with true good will, seeks to be His alone.

ASPIRATION –

Sweet Infant Jesus, come and open the door of mercy to sinful men.

Form your resolution!

Some things to ponder:
Advent is a time of preparation. It prepares us for Christmas, but it also prepares us for Christ's second coming. Advent is the beginning of the Church's liturgical year. The themes of Advent have always focused on preparing the way of the Lord, on repentance, and on the role of Mary in salvation history. Margaret Anna Cusack touches upon these themes in a most beautiful way through her Advent meditations. She draws us into the Heart of the Infant Jesus and reminds us of our Christian call to preparation. She helps us to focus on how to prepare ourselves for Christ's coming among us as man, reminding us that our hearts are to be grateful, prayerful, and full of repentance.

Ask yourself:
What image that Margaret Anna presents in her meditations helps me to focus on the meaning of Advent? In her meditations, do I see a progression of movement in the themes for Advent? How are we to make progress during the weeks of Advent? After meditating upon Margaret Anna Cusack's reflections, what do I feel God calling me to do during this Advent season? How can I make this a truly holy season of preparation in my spiritual life?

Let us pray:
Grant your faithful, we pray, almighty God, the resolve to run forth to meet your Christ with righteous deeds at his coming, so that, gathered at his right hand, they may be worthy to possess the heavenly Kingdom, through our Lord Jesus Christ, your Son, Who lives and reigns with you in the Unity of the Holy Spirit, One God, Forever and ever.
Amen.
(from the Roman Missal, First Sunday of Advent)

Christmas Day, Christmas Week, and Epiphany

Christmas Day

"…she gave birth to her firstborn son. She wrapped him in swaddling clothes and laid him in a manger…"
(Luke 2:7)

"For when peaceful stillness encompassed everything
and the night in its swift course was half spent,
Your all-powerful word from heaven's royal throne
leapt into the doomed land…"
(Wisdom 18:14)

"…Open to me, my sister, my friend,
my dove, my perfect one!
For my head is wet with dew,
my hair, with the moisture of the night…"
(Canticle 5:2)

First Point –

Today we can have only one thought and one subject; our prelude is our meditation, and our meditation our prelude. "She brought forth her first-born son, and laid Him in a manger." O sweet Mary, bring Him forth tonight also, and lay Him in the little manger of our hearts. They are very lifeless and very cold, but thou wilt try to warm them for Jesus, your first-born. We have tried to prepare a lodging for Him, and poor as it is, we know He will accept it, if you will come with Him. We must try to make reparation to you also, sweet Mother, for the unkindness of your children, who keep the warm house for themselves, and drive you to the stable. Alas! Sweet Mother, how many are there now who are as cold and as cruel to you? And as you did tell Saint Gertrude that we are all your children, that Jesus is called your first-born, rather than first-begotten, because you will include us all in your family, and give us all a share in your maternal love, so we must act towards you as children, and you will act towards us as a mother.

SECOND POINT –

Consider the time at which Jesus comes: in the night, when all things are in "quiet silence." Yes, Jesus always comes to us in the night of sorrow, and when our hearts are still. But our silence must be a quiet silence if we desire to entertain this gentle child, for He cannot bear the rough noise of unquiet men, or the busy-talk activity of a heart exteriorly silent but unworldly and full of commotion within. Oh! If we will but quiet our hearts and open them wide, He will "leap from His royal throne" into the midst of them, so great is His haste to come and save us! Nay, He even asks us to open them for Him, and who could refuse anything to the little Babe of Bethlehem? He calls us "His sister and His love," He even tries to persuade Himself that we are His "undefiled," and He comes with His head full of dew, full of the rich dew of the graces of His unity, that He may fertilize our souls; but He comes also wet with the drops of the night, with the grief and tears of His adorable Humanity. O little Babe of Bethlehem, come, leap into our hearts tonight. We will treasure the dew You bring, and we will try to wipe away the "drops of the night" from Your baby brow, and we will shut the doors of our hearts so close once You come, that You will never be able to leave them again.

THIRD POINT –

Let us try to enter into the spirit and intentions of the Church, as she celebrates three times the adorable sacrifice on this great festival. She commemorates thereby the threefold salvation He has come to effect: first, He saves those who lived before the Law was given; second, He saves those who were under the Law; and thirdly, He saves those under the gospel. And further, three spiritual nativities are commemorated: first, the eternal nativity of Christ, born before all time, from eternity, of His Father; second, His nativity in time from the womb of Mary; and third, His spiritual birth by grace in the souls of His children. Hence, we do well to offer the Midnight Mass in thanksgiving to God for the eternal generation of His only begotten son—offering to the sweet Infant Jesus all the love and sanctity of those who lived and served Him faithfully before the Law was given, and praying specifically for all who are in mortal sin. The second Mass, at break of day, is in thanksgiving for His love in coming down into the womb of Mary. It is thanksgiving for her perfect purity, and it offers Him all the love and devotion of those who served Him faithfully under the law, and prays for those whom He is leading from darkness into light, that their entrance into the Church may be hastened. Lastly, we offer the Mass at mid-day, in thanksgiving for His love for us and for all whom He has permitted to live in the full light of the gospel; and in thanksgiving for His exceeding love in abiding with us in our very souls, as He prays fervently for all the just on earth.

Aspiration –

*O my sweet Infant Jesus, I love You, and because I love You,
I am sorry that I have offended You.
Make a Christmas offering of your best resolution to the
little Babe of Bethlehem.*

Examen.

December 26th

Feast of Saint Stephen

The Heart of the Infant Jesus Came to Offer Itself to the Eternal Father and to Suffer

"…so I said, 'See; I come
with an inscribed scroll written upon me.
I delight to do your will, my God;
your law is in my inner being!'"

(Psalm 40:8–9)

FIRST PRELUDE –

Consider the Infant Jesus at the moment of His birth, offering Himself to the External Father, that He might do His will.

SECOND PRELUDE –

Pray, through the merits of this sweet Infant, that you may offer yourself up entirely to the Divine Will.

FIRST POINT –

Consider the words, "Behold I come." They are the words of one who comes willingly, of one who comes authoritatively. Jesus comes willingly, because He desires our salvation more than we can possibly imagine; He comes with authority, because He comes as God. But how does He come? Let us look at the crib, and we shall see. He comes not as a mighty King or a victorious conqueror; He comes not as we would have expected a God to come. His appearance so little betokens His greatness that it is a stumbling block and a scandal to His people, even as His hiddenness in the Blessed Sacrament still continues to be, for He comes as a little child, to teach us humility and to win our love.

SECOND POINT –

For what purpose does He come? He tells us Himself: "In the head of the book it is written of me that I should do your will." This is the one purpose of Jesus in the Incarnation, and this should be our one and only purpose in life. In proportion as we have no other purpose will be the degree of our sanctity and the measure of our reward. Oh, how grand, how noble is the soul which has only this one purpose in life! We see every day what great things men can effect who concentrate their energies on one occupation, who give themselves entirely to one study. We see, alas! too often, what men gain for earth who never allow themselves to be diverted from an end, who employ every moment of time and every facility of mind for this end. We see how ingenious they become in converting the most opposite and unlikely circumstances to their own advantage. O sweet Infant Jesus, make us as wise and as ingenious, concentrating all our energies on one end, in employing all our facilities for one purpose.

THIRD POINT –

We cannot do the will of another without sacrifice, and this is precisely the reason why so many fail in this oneness of purpose which is so necessary for the attainment of great sanctity. Jesus did not accomplish His Father's will without sacrifice. He has already begun to suffer, and in a few days He will even shed His blood sooner than fail in the accomplishment of that will. How can we bear to see an infant bleeding beneath the knife of circumcision, in obedience to an ordinance which He came to abolish, while we cannot bear to do what causes us a little inconvenience, even to fulfill a momentous duty? The truth is, we are unwilling to sacrifice ourselves, and until we are willing to do God's will in self-sacrifice, we cannot be like our Infant Jesus! But it is not necessary that we should like self-sacrifice. Humanly speaking, Saint Stephen did not like the stones which sent him to heaven, but he liked God's will better than his own; it was God's will that he should be stoned and Stephen preferred being stoned, not because He liked it, but because it was God's will. Oh, let us only bear the rough stones of pain and adversity because they are God's will, and we, like Stephen, shall see heaven open, and Jesus waiting there to crown us.

Aspiration –

O Sweet Infant Jesus, help me to do Your will.

Form your resolution!
Examen.

December 27th

Feast of Saint John the Evangelist

The Heart of the Infant Jesus Teaching Us How to be His Friends

"You are my friends if you do what I command you."
(John 15:14)

FIRST PRELUDE –

Behold the Little Infant Jesus in the manger, asking us to be His friends.

SECOND PRELUDE –

Tell Him, with your whole heart's love, that you love Him, and that you have no words to tell Him how much.

- Pause and Reflect -

FIRST POINT –

But there is an even higher degree of love and perfection than that of merely submitting to the will of God. No doubt we shall be very perfect if we submit to the will of God; but we shall be very saintly if we love it. Saint John loved it more than any human words can tell, when he knew that Jesus willed him to suffer all the pains of martyrdom, and then, when he had suffered all he could suffer, saved him, by a miracle, from temporal death. Oh, what tears Saint John wept upon the Heart of Jesus, when he found himself so near heaven, and yet forbidden to enter it! But his tears were tears of burning love. There was no unwillingness to accept the will of his Beloved, for he and Jesus were friends, such friends as never had been, as never will be. O blessed John, plead for us with your Friend Jesus, that our wills may become one with Him, as yours was.

Second Point –

Saint John knew what he was sacrificing, when his friend Jesus said he must not go home after that martyrdom which almost opened the gates of heaven for him. He knew the long life that was before Him; he knew that many, many years must pass before he could lie again upon the bosom of Jesus, as he had once lain; but John wished what Jesus wished, because they were friends and if earthly friends do not act contrary to their inclinations to please each other, but even scarcely know when they sacrifice themselves for each other, how much more must it be possible when Jesus becomes so united to a soul, that it ceases to have a will, and sacrifice becomes a joy! The friendship between Jesus and John was perfect. It was the nearest love to the love between Mary and Jesus. Jesus lay on the bosom of Mary, and John lay on the bosom of Jesus, and as he had once lain there corporally at the last supper, so to the end of his life he lay there mystically, and hence could not choose but prefer the will of his friend Jesus, whatever that will might be.

Third Point –

Let us pray to the blessed Evangelist to obtain this perfect love for us. The love of submission is very holy, but the love of union is the most sublime perfection. The love of submission kisses the hand of Jesus, and accepts whatever He sends; but the love of union lies in His bosom, it feels the pulsation of His heart, it knows His will almost by instinct; because His will is so mysteriously its own, that it has ceased to have an individual will or instinct; and even if the hand that caressed it struck it to the very soul, and pierced a thousand swords into its inmost bring, it would still have no will but to accept and to prefer all the will of its Beloved.

ASPIRATION –

O blessed John, lying upon the bosom of Jesus your friend, pray for us, that we also may be His friends, by doing whatever He commands us.

Form your resolution!
Examen.

December 28th

Feast of the Holy Innocents

*"A voice was heard in Ramah,
sobbing and loud lamentation;
Rachel weeping for her children,
and she would not be consoled,
since they were no more."*

(Matthew 2:18)

FIRST PRELUDE –

Consider the grief of the mothers on earth, and the joy of the children in heaven.

SECOND PRELUDE –

Pray that you may be ever ready to adore the designs of Providence, however mysterious.

- Pause and Reflect -

FIRST POINT –

Consider the anguish of those poor mothers, who could see nothing in the designs of God but a dark, cold, dreadful severity. They would not be comforted, and hence there could be but little, if any, submission in their grief. They were compelled to submit to the will of God, perhaps because they would only submit by compulsion, and yet, even for them this compulsion is mercy and love. They know now what their children have gained by being sacrificed for

Jesus. His Infant Blood has been shed for them and they are the first fruits of the virgins and martyrs purchased by that Blood. Oh, could those mothers only see the end as well as the beginning of their course would they not almost offer their children themselves to the word of the destroyer? But there is another mother already preparing to offer her Child to the cruel life of suffering, freely, generously, even while her heart is wrought with anguish; and by that offering she will make reparation for the sin and rebellion of many a mother who refuses to give God the treasures for which He asks.

Second Point –

Consider how awful a thing it is to oblige God to compel our submission. We cannot hinder the accomplishment of His Divine Will, even in the very slightest matter; hence submission is our wisest as well as our holiest course. If we cannot submit because we believe that all which He ordains is ordered for us with the tenderest love, as well as with the most consummate wisdom, at least let us submit beneath the mighty hand of God. But, O sweet Infant Jesus, we would rather submit for love—no, we will not even talk of submission, for who that loves ever names that word when there is question of the desires of those they love being accomplished by them, however painful? We will rather unite our wills so entirely to You, that we shall cease to have wills of our own, and hence there will be no need of submission to what we ourselves desire.

Third Point –

God never takes anything away from us without some purpose of exceeding love. All we want for our peace of mind is to believe that "God is love." Alas! That it should be so necessary to try and persuade ourselves of it, even at this blessed season, with the Infant Jesus so near us. Were not those tried and afflicted mothers incomparably more profound by God than other mothers whose children were left to them, and who, when they grew up, cried out, "Crucify Him! Crucify Him!" and, perhaps, helped to slay their Lord in act as well as in will? If the mothers who "would not be comforted" loved God as every creature should love Him, they would not have refused to be comforted; for He would have been their comfort, even while they wept, as Jesus permits us to weep when He sends us anguish and affliction.

ASPIRATION –

Heart of my Infant Jesus, hide me in You!

Form your resolution!
Examen.

December 29th

The Heart of the Infant Receiving the Adoration of the Angels

"And suddenly there was a multitude of the heavenly host with the angel, praising God and saying:
'Glory to God in the highest
and on earth peace to those on whom his favor rests.'"
(Luke 2:13–14)

FIRST PRELUDE –

Consider the night of the Nativity, and behold the angels appearing in the sky, chanting their glorious hymn.

SECOND PRELUDE –

Pray for the grace of thankfulness, that you may truly glorify God in every circumstance of your life.

- Pause and Reflect -

FIRST POINT –

Let us consider the words of the angels, "Glory to God in the highest." The first thought, the first desire of those blessed spirits, is the glory of God. Their own interest and their own glory never for a moment occupies their minds. Hence, so long as God is glorified, they do not concern themselves further. Their love is the love of union, and they know no will but God's will. It matters not to them that the fallen angels are left in chains and darkness, and that Jesus has passed by their nature to redeem and save ours. No thought can occupy these blessed spirits for one moment but the great one of God's glory. They only desire what glorifies Him most, and they know that He is most glorified by the salvation of man, because He has willed it so. When shall we learn to imitate their noble disinterestedness? When shall we attain this perfection? When shall we be content and even give thanks to God, when others are advanced, either temporally or spiritually, and we passed over?

SECOND POINT –

Peace is the necessary consequence of this love of union, which only desires God's glory; and it is people of good will, alone, who truly desire it. Oh, let us pray for a good will, a loving will, a perfect will. Let us ask to have a will like the will of the Little Infant Jesus. He came because His Father willed it, He is man because His Father willed it, and every action of His adorable humanity is done purely and simply because His Father wills it. Above all things, we need pure wills and simple wills. A pure will is like a sparkling stream of crystal water flowing from its source to its end; a simple will is like the line of beauty, beautiful because of its simplicity. How full of fervor are those souls whose wills are pure and simple. They have no self-interest to disturb their tranquility, for we are seldom disturbed unless by some self-interest. Even if they suffer, they are full of peace. No amount of interior trial, however harrowing—no amount of dark temptations, no distressing thoughts, perhaps one of the keenest trials of some souls—can for a moment really disturb their peace, for they will to suffer because their Beloved wills it and hence they are not disturbed or disquieted.

Third Point –

We never lose our peace, unless we desire to possess something which we have not got, or to retain something which we are afraid of losing. But the soul which has advanced to the love of union neither wishes to possess or to retain. She is content to be deprived of all but her love and her God, and even this she does not ask to possess sensibly. Oh, how full of God, and how dear to Him, is a soul this advanced in sanctity! Truly she is full of peace, because she is absolutely united to the God of Peace. If we desire this perfection, let us ask it of the Heart of the Infant Jesus; let us offer His disposition to the Eternal Father, that ours may be renewed and perfected; let us constantly offer ourselves to God, in union with the oblation of the Infant Jesus.

Aspiration –

Heart of the Infant Jesus, unite me wholly to Yourself.

Form your resolution!
Examen.

December 30th

The Heart of the Infant Jesus, Receiving the Visit of the Shepherds

"So they went in haste and found Mary and Joseph, and the infant lying in the manger."
(Luke 2:16)

FIRST PRELUDE –

Consider these good and holy shepherds listening to the music of the angels, and then hastening to Bethlehem to adore their Infant King.

SECOND PRELUDE –

How good and holy these dear shepherds must have been, whom our Lord selected, in preference to all others, for this vision of angels and this marvelous announcement! We may well believe it was not without a special design of Providence. Perhaps it was because the poor and the unlearned are always more ready to believe than the rich, who are hardened by their riches, or the learned, who are blinded by their pride. Perhaps it was because Jesus came to proclaim the gospel to the poor as the fittest subjects for the eternal kingdom. Who can imagine their simple joy, their lively faith, their ardent devotion? Those who have been privileged to be much with the poor of a truly Catholic country, can best imagine and realize what these shepherds did and said that Christmas night. They caught the accents of the angels, "Glory to God!" and they handed down that sublime song of praise to those who came after them, that they might utter it, even to the end of time, even in circumstances of the deepest suffering.

First Point –

Consider the haste of the shepherds. They did not pause to consider whether their flocks would be safe if they left them. Ah, no! The Lamb of God was dearer to them than the little lambs and sheep, which were their worldly all. They did not stay to consult whether the vision of the angels was imagination or reality. They simply believed, and believing they loved, and loving they hastened, and they had their reward, for they found Mary and Joseph, and the Infant, and it was all they desired. They had their reward, for they were privileged to be the first to behold and adore their newborn King. Oh, with what love the Sweet Infant Jesus greeted them! How He stretched out His little hands to welcome them, while Mary told them all that Jesus wished her to say!

Second Point –

Perhaps the shepherds represented Christ's priests as well as His poor, and perhaps He called them first, as the pastors of His flock were called to minister to His people. How we should honour and love the shepherds of God's Church! How we should respect their absolute self-renunciation! They leave their flocks; that is, all their earthly wealth and convenience; to minister to the Lamb of God in the persons of His sheep. They most truly honour the Incarnation of the Son of God by their continued oblation of His Body and Blood, and, like the shepherds, they spend their lives in making known His wonders and His love. O sweet Infant Jesus, we would come also with the shepherds to your crib. We would come with the poor and simple, and believe with them and be like them. May we also find Mary and

Joseph, and the Infant, and may they place You in our hearts to reside therein forever.

ASPIRATION –

O my Sweet Infant Jesus, I love You, and because I love You, I am sorry that I have offended You.

Form your resolution!
Examen.

December 31ˢᵗ

The Heart of the Infant Jesus, Enlightening His Blessed Mother In all the Mysteries of His Life and His Love

"And Mary kept all these things, reflecting on them in her heart."

(Luke 2:19)

FIRST PRELUDE –

Consider the tender and reverential love with which Mary watches every movement of her Infant Son, and considers all the circumstances connected with His Life.

SECOND PRELUDE –

Pray for grace to ponder on the things of God, as Mary did.

- Pause and Reflect -

FIRST POINT –

"Mary kept all these words, pondering them in her heart." In order to ponder on the words of God, we must "keep them." Now, keeping implies guarding closely in a secure place. We must, then, treasure up the words of Jesus in our hearts; we must have a large space there to lay them up in; and in order to find room for them, we must expel all other words—all idle words, all curious words, above all, every sinful word. Let us commence the New Year by imitating our Blessed Mother in this. If we keep the words of God like Mary, we shall also ponder them, in our measure, like Mary. How reverently, and carefully, we should ponder all the circumstances of the life of our divine Lord; how we should linger over every word He uttered! Those who devote themselves to this keeping and pondering on those things will learn a thousand secrets of love which will never be manifested to the thoughtless and those who are less occupied with God.

Second Point –

Let us consider Mary as the first model and example of the practice of holy meditation. The first meditation on the life of Jesus was made by Mary in the stable at Bethlehem, beside the crib, and hence it is that those who are most devout to her attain a special grace of knowing and understanding the mysteries of the life of Jesus. How simple and how sublime was that meditation! The creature adored and meditated upon the Creator, and the Creator poured forth light and love into the heart of the creature. This is the essence of all true meditation. If we were more simple we should find less difficulty in practicing it. Meditation on our side is thinking about Jesus as we would think over the words and acts of a friend whom we love very much, and mental prayer, which should always accompany meditation, is asking the friend we love for what we want. Even in the sublime prayer of the love of union the soul asks love instinctively, though the voice of the soul has ceased to make itself heard. Meditation on the part of God is a pouring forth on us by sight to know, and to love to do His will; and this is given in proportion to our earnestness. Souls who live very near God, and think of Him constantly, are ever receiving this light and love, which guides them and purifies their intention in a marvelous manner, even in the most trifling actions.

THIRD POINT –

O Mary, pondering at the crib of Jesus, teach me how to ponder on His love and His mercies, teach me how to ponder on all the favours and graces He has granted me during the past year, until the flame of thanksgiving breaks forth in my heart and manifests itself in songs of love and adoration. Teach me how to ponder on all my sins and ingratitude, on my wicked misuse of these mercies; on my sinful neglect of His inspirations; on my evil failure to correspond with the countless lights He has given me; on my frequent refusal to listen to the murmurs of His love; on my neglect in observing the sweet practice of devotion He has taught me. Teach me to pour forth my whole soul in tears of grief and look upon my Infant God lying in your arms, and ask Him to forgive me, for He can refuse you nothing. Obtain for me the grace to give my whole being to His service, and to make a solemn consecration of myself to Him for the New Year in the stable of Bethlehem. Oh, may the angels who witness my oblation, obtain for me the grace to keep my promise!

ASPIRATION –

Heart of my Infant Jesus, have mercy. Mother of Jesus, be my Mother.

Form your resolution!
Examen.

January 1st

Feast of the Circumcision

"When eight days were completed for his circumcision, he was named Jesus, the name given him by the angel before he was conceived in the womb."
(Luke 2:21)

FIRST PRELUDE –

Consider the devotion of Mary at this ceremony, and the tenderness with which she tries to console her suffering child.

SECOND PRELUDE –

Pray that you may be ever ready to sympathize in the sufferings of Jesus by meditation, by your own sufferings, and by compassionating the sufferings of others.

- Pause and Reflect -

FIRST POINT –

Let us begin the year with our Little Jesus, even though He should ask us to suffer with Him. Let us begin it by offering Him a New Year's gift of all our love. Let us salute Him the moment we awake in the morning, and wish Him, for His New Year's joy, the conversion of countless souls, and the increased sanctification of all His elect. Today our Dear Lord receives the sweet name of Jesus. Let us salute Him by His new name continually. He has already revealed to Saint Gertrude that however great the unworthiness of those who utter aspirations of love, He is pleased with them, since a vase of sweet perfume gives forth its odors, no matter how vile the stick which may be used to stir it up. Oh, let us stir up the perfumes of love in the Heart of our little Jesus all day long with the tenderest forms of prayer.

SECOND POINT –

If we would be the children of our Sweet Infant King, we must be content to be like Him. He was made in all things "like unto His brethren" (Hebrews 2:17). Are we content to be made like our Brother Jesus? Do we wish to be made like our Brother Jesus? Do we desire more than we desire anything else in the world, to be made like our Brother Jesus? O sweet Jesus, we do desire it! But we have seen the knife with which our Brother was wounded, and we shrink back in fear. Oh, help us, Sweet Jesus; we desire to be like You, but we shrink from suffering, although we know that unless we suffer we cannot be like You! Your life commences with suffering, with, we might almost say, unnecessary suffering; for the circumcision was not necessary for our salvation, since one drop of Your Blood could save us; but one of the many mysteries which we cannot "know" here but which we shall "know here after" (John 13:7) is the mystery of what seems to us unnecessary suffering. The life of Jesus is full of this mystery—blessed are they whose lives are made like Him in this also, for though even the most saintly must say, and say truly, "and we indeed [suffer] justly, for we receive the just reward of our deeds, but this man has done no evil" (Luke 23:41); yet there are souls who seem to suffer more than others, perhaps as the highest reward of a more than ordinary sanctity.

Third Point –

But there is a special kind of suffering, of which Mary is the great exemplar. Jesus is the cause of her suffering as well as the cause of her joy. Blessed are they who are privileged to follow her in this mystic path of sanctity! This grace is given, in its highest degree, to those favored souls who suffer purely for Jesus, who are privileged to share in the mysteries of His passion, and, in a lower degree of sanctity, in the sufferings of His daily life. It is also granted, in a certain measure, to those who suffer for or on account of others. In whatever degree this privilege is granted to us, let us unite ourselves to Mary. We may never be permitted to share, however little, in the pains of Calvary, but we may in our measure share in the suffering life of Jesus. Let us commence the New Year with a generous offering of ourselves to bear all His love may ask.

Aspiration –

Heart of my Infant Jesus, be my home for the coming year.

Form your resolution, and make a generous offering to do and to suffer the will of God during the New Year in union with the suffering and obedience of the Infant Jesus.
Examen.

Liturgical Note — When Margaret Anna Cusack was alive, January 1st would have been the Feast of the Circumcision of the Lord. After Vatican II, New Year's Day was given to the Feast of Mary, Mother of God, a holy day of obligation, which is observed today. There is no longer a feast to celebrate the Circumcision of the Lord, but the meaning behind the feast is observed on January 3rd, The Feast of the Holy Name of Jesus; and on February 2nd, The Presentation of the Lord in the Temple. It is interesting to note that Margaret Anna makes reference to

Mary, the Mother of God, on this day, even before it would be observed as a feast, as well as making mention of the honor of the Holy Name of Jesus. This shows the Nun of Kenmare's keen insight into the meaning of this feast which is now observed on the first day of the year.

Some things to ponder:
Throughout her Christmas meditations, Margaret Anna Cusack reveals the meaning behind the season: it is to prepare a place in our hearts, that we may welcome the Infant Jesus into our lives. Throughout the meditations she gives examples of how this can be done: by giving glory to God, as the angels did; by expressing it through love, as Saint John did in his friendship with Jesus; and through sacrifice, as Saint Stephen did through his martyrdom. Of course the ultimate sacrifice, as Margaret Anna makes mention of, is through our participation at Mass. In all of her meditations there is an emphasis on Mary's role in the Christmas story, for Mary is to be our example of how we welcome the Christ Child into our lives. My personal favorite of the Christmas meditations is the one for December 30th. Here she uses the example of the shepherds as a model of this love and sacrifice, for they gave glory to God and went in haste to the stable to pay homage and respect to the newborn King.

Let us ask ourselves:
How do we prepare a place for the Infant Jesus to enter into our lives? How can Mary be an example to us as we celebrate the Christmas season? Which Christmas meditation of Margaret Anna's is your favorite and why?

Let us pray:
O God, who makes us glad with the yearly remembrance of the birth of your only Son Jesus Christ: Grant that as we joyfully receive him for our Redeemer so we may with sure confidence behold Him when He shall come to be our

Judge, who lives and reigns with you, with the Holy Spirit, one God, world without end.
Amen.
(from the [Protestant] Book of Common Prayer)

The Feast of Epiphany

The Adoration of the Magi

"…behold, magi from the east arrived in Jerusalem, saying, 'Where is the newborn king of the Jews? We saw his star at its rising and have come to do him homage.'"
(Matthew 2:1–2)

First Prelude –

Consider the holy anxiety with which these Wise Men seek the newborn King.

Second Prelude –

Pray that you may be always ready to come to Jesus whenever and however He calls you.

- Pause and Reflect -

First Point –

Consider the faith of these wise men. They do not come to ascertain if there is such a person born as one calling himself the King of the Jews; they do not come to make scrupulous and captious investigations about the revelation they have received; no, their faith is sublime in its simplicity; they believe, and they worship. They believe the revelation; therefore they act on the revelation. How happy should we be if our faith were equally practical! But, alas! We believe coldly, and hence we act coldly. We give a careless assent to the most important truths, and hence they have but little influence on our daily conduct. Oh, let us pray with our whole hearts for a lively faith. Let us employ ourselves constantly in making Acts of Faith. Repeated acts will strengthen a habit, whether for good or evil, more than all the reflections we can make; and these reflections are only of value in helping us to reduce evil acts and produce good ones. Let us, then, reflect on the faith, that we may be led to act on the faith; and by acting on it, be confirmed in it.

Second Point –

Today we shall consider especially the great value and importance of the gift of faith. No considerations of ours can possibly impress us with its importance; no words can explain its value. Faith alone can teach us to estimate faith, since all that is of faith can only be appreciated by a supernaturally enlightened mind. Let us for a moment suppose that God had not called the Gentiles to the light of faith, and that He had come only or especially for the salvation of the Jews, His own chosen people; let us suppose, even though the treasures of faith have been opened to all, that we had been born heathens; let us suppose that we had been born even of Christian parents, and yet not in the true church: might we not have been placed in any of these circumstances, if God had ordered our position in life other than it has been? And have we ever been sufficiently thankful to God for all He has done for us?

Third Point –

Our lives should prove our thankfulness. The Magi showed their thankfulness for God's call by their fervour in obeying it. Do we live as if we had the gift of faith? Are our lives the lives of those who believe in God? Alas! Are we not every day acting in direct opposition to our faith, living as if we believed this life to be our only concern, while we say daily, "I believe in the life everlasting"; living as if temporal things were our great object, when we believe that in a few short years they will have passed away, and a long eternity will open on us; when the things of time will be unimportant, except as regards their relation to the things of eternity, as a mere second is to a century? Do we not believe that to receive the Body and Blood of Jesus is the greatest grace, the most stupendous favour which can be conferred on any mortal, and, alas! do we not act, again and again, as if the merest trifles were far more important? Do we not fret and distract ourselves about the trifles of daily life, although we know that we shall, hereafter, only remember our earthly life's greatest afflictions as the light shadows of a summer day? Oh, for more faith—more real, earnest faith, or rather, oh, for more love of Jesus, and less love of self; and then we should soon live lives of greater faith, for if we believe we shall love, and if we love, we shall act on our belief.

Aspiration –

Heart of my Infant King, help me to love You, and to live for You.

Form your resolution!
Examen.

Second Meditation

The Feast of Epiphany
On True Worship

"They prostrated themselves and did him homage."
(Matthew 2:11)

First Prelude –

Consider the love and zeal with which these holy men prostrated themselves before the Infant Jesus.

Second Prelude –

Endeavor to imitate their example by fervent adoration of the Word Made Flesh.

- Pause and Reflect -

First Point –

Consider the example of the wise men: "And falling down, they adored Him." How sublime is their faith! They see only a poor mother and a poor child, yet they never hesitate for a moment nor make outward circumstances an excuse for unbelief. How the Heart of the Infant Jesus must have been consoled by this adoration! What favours and graces He must have prepared to reward these good kings! How Mary thanked them in her heart, and how she rejoiced that even a few of God's creatures came to pay Him homage! Already our dear Lord foresees the mockery of His long night of trial, when the knees of His creatures will be bent to Him, not to honour Him, but to revile Him. Already He beholds the crowds through which He will pass, where none will offer Him the least mark of respect. Already He beholds the faithful before His tabernacle, cold and careless, as if God were not present there, and the faithless mocking and blaspheming in His very presence. But with all this knowledge, He lies still in Mary's arms, and never even breathes one desire to return to His Father's courts, where millions upon millions of angels adore Him, and love as they adore. What a lesson to us of perseverance in well-doing, through all discouragements!

Second Point –

Let us try to imitate the example of our sweet Jesus. We measure our success too much by what appears exteriorly, and too little by the judgment of God. Hence, we are easily discouraged if our plans are thwarted or fail, whereas we should continue our work, whatever it may be; waiting for God's time of prosperity should He will it to prosper, and remaining more than content with failure, if He wills it to fail. How little we know the real meaning of the words 'failure' and 'success'! Did not the Incarnation look like a failure at Bethlehem and Calvary? Does it not often look like a failure now, when we see so little fruit from it? And yet it is the masterpiece of Eternal Wisdom, of Wisdom which can neither fail in design nor in execution.

Third Point –

Let us try to console our sweet Jesus by offering Him the adoration of the Wise Men, and by our own adorations. Whenever we hear the words "Oh, come let us adore Him," so often repeated by the Church at this holy season, let us prostrate in spirit if not bodily, and adore our Infant King.

How much we lose by performing such acts of adoration mechanically and without a special intention! We kneel before the Blessed Sacrament many times in the day, without a thought, without a definite purpose. If each time we knelt we had the intention in our minds of offering the action to console the Infant Jesus for the neglect of His creatures, how it would gladden His divine Heart! If we offered it to atone for the neglect of the Blessed Sacrament, even if we failed to remember our purpose each time through human frailty, it would at least be very consoling to our dear Lord to see that we have the intention. Christmas is a season of the richest graces; do not let it pass without obtaining all our newborn King is willing to give.

ASPIRATION –

Sweet Jesus, I adore and I love You for all who do not adore and love You.

Form your resolution!
Examen.

Something to ponder:
Margaret Anna Cusack wrote several meditations about the Feast of the Epiphany, which is another important celebration during the Christmas Season. The word 'epiphany' means a manifestation, and Our Lord manifested, or revealed Himself, to the nations represented by the Wise Men, also known as the Kings from the East. Margaret Anna reflects on how these Wise Men are, like the shepherds, examples of faith for us. The Wise Men did not question what the star was, but they searched and responded, acting in faith. They show us that the treasure of faith has been opened to all of us in this manifestation of Christ to the Gentiles. This manifestation then leads the Wise Men to pay homage and adoration to the Infant King who is God. My favorite line that Margaret Anna Cusack reflects upon is when

she tells us to not let this season pass us by without seeking the graces it offers. This is the example of the Wise Men: in their search they discovered a treasure of graces in the newborn King.

Ask yourself:
What are some things that I question in my faith? Why is it hard to believe without seeing? How can the Feast of the Epiphany help me in my search for faith? What can I do during Christmas to experience the grace of God?

Let us pray:
Jesus, as we travel far and fast, lead our minds back to the Wise Men following Your star, and forward to the day when all will see Your shining light. Jesus, Light of the World, let Your bright star stand over the place where the poor have to live; lead our sages to wisdom and our rulers to reverence. O God, by the leading of a star You revealed Your Son Jesus Christ to the Gentiles. Grant that Your Church may be a light to the nations, so that the whole world may come to see the splendor of Your glory, through Jesus Christ our Lord.
(A New Zealand Prayer Book)

The Five Sundays of Lent and Holy Week

Ash Wednesday

The Heart of Jesus, Going Alone Into the Wilderness

"Then Jesus was led by the Spirit into the desert to be tempted by the devil."

(Matthew 4:1)

First Prelude –

Consider Jesus going alone into the desert.

Second Prelude –

Pray that you may have the grace to follow Him ever closer.

- Pause and Reflect -

First Point –

Consider how our sweet Jesus prepares himself for the three years of His public life: He goes alone into the desert. Thus it is that when He calls any favoured soul to a greater nearness to Himself, He sends her into the desert. Friends die, or forsake her; the dearest ties are broken, and she is left alone. Well for her if she sits not down to weep by the wayside, but rises courageously and follows where Jesus calls. Have you been called into the desert by special severance from friends and home? Has God broken the ties that bind you in the charms of human love, or have you yourself, with heroic courage, severed yourself from all? And if it be so, are you courageously facing the perils of the desert?

SECOND POINT –

Consider Who it is that leads us into the desert. It is Jesus. He has Himself walked the same path, He knows its difficulties and its dangers. Let us cling to Him or if our spiritual vision be so clouded that we cannot discern His presence, let us at least look for His foot marks on the way, and follow where He has walked. There is no wavering, no uncertainty, no retracing of steps. On then, with courage, into the desert: the desert of retirement, which at this holy season we are bound to practice; the desert of prayer, where we may find only auditing and desolation, but to which we are now especially called; the desert of temptation if such should be the Divine Will; and consider how few there are who are not tempted at some period of their spiritual life.

THIRD POINT –

Consider how you may console the Heart of Jesus, going alone into the wilderness. The best consolation that you can give Him will be to profit by what He has suffered for you. Endeavor each day during this holy season to meditate more deeply on His suffering life on earth. All that He has endured, even to the most trifling circumstance, had not only a deep meaning and an infinite merit, but it is intended also for our example and instruction. In proportion as we endeavor to enter into, and imitate, the life of Christ on earth, our sanctity will increase, and our reward for all eternity will accumulate an exceeding weight of glory. Say, then, three Our Fathers in honor of this mystery, offering them to the Eternal Father for all who are in doubt and perplexity as to their vocation; and to obtain for yourself the grace to withdraw courageously from all that might hinder you from a closer union with your Lord during this penitential season, and for all who are preparing for holy orders.

ASPIRATION:

Heart of Jesus Crucified, give me the grace to follow wherever You lead.

Thursday After Ash Wednesday

The Heart of Jesus, Tempted In the Wilderness

(cf. Matthew 4)

FIRST PRELUDE –

Consider Jesus preparing for temptation.

SECOND PRELUDE –

Pray that you may have the grace to foresee, and prepare for, moments of danger.

- Pause and Reflect -

FIRST POINT –

May we not reverently suppose that Jesus prepares for temptation by prayer? He needs it not. He cannot yield one shadow of consent, and yet we know that before His passion, so long foreseen and accepted, His agony of prayer ends in a sweat of Blood. Oh my Jesus, You pray, You agonize in Your prayer, and I, miserable that I am, how do I pray? A few cold words, carelessly said and soon almost forgotten; and I expect to be answered, to be succored in temptation as if I had agonized with You.

SECOND POINT –

Consider the necessity of preparing for temptation. We will perhaps acknowledge that it is necessary, but do we really act on our conviction? There are temptations to little faults which have become so habitual to us that we scarcely notice them. There are sudden, overwhelming, almost instantaneous temptations to which we may in a moment yield, and in that moment peril our eternal salvation. What daily preparation do we make for such awful contingencies? If we have prepared, if we have asked for the grace beforehand, we may hope that however sudden the temptation may be the needful succor will anticipate it; but if we have not asked, can we hope even to rise quickly after our fall?

THIRD POINT –

Consider how you may console the Heart of Jesus preparing for temptation. It is for you that He endures these bitter trials, it is for you that He condescends to bear this anguish, that you, through His victory, may obtain grace to conquer in your hour of need. Oh! If we but used these mysteries of love and sorrow as our Divine Lord intended we should; if we availed ourselves of the fortitude, of the grace He has purchased so dearly for us, how much holier our lives would be. Each individual suffering in the life of our Divine Lord obtained some special grace for us, and in a special manner for the transgressions we commit when under similar trial. Let us learn to use these treasures of divine grace as we should, for ourselves and for others. Offer to the Eternal Father again and again the infinite merit and condescension of the Heart of Jesus in suffering Himself to be tempted, and pray that for His sake you may obtain pardon and contrition for having yielded so often to the slightest trial of your virtue, and ask for strength to resist in the future. Say one Our Father and one Hail Mary to console the Heart of Jesus, preparing for temptation, and to obtain strength to resist whatever temptation you find it most difficult to conquer; pray also for all who are tempted in any way to resist inspirations for a more perfect life.

ASPIRATION –

Heart of Jesus, tempted for love of me, help me to resist temptation for love of You.

Friday after Ash Wednesday

The Heart of Jesus, Tempted and Alone

"Then was Jesus led by the Spirit into the desert…"
(Matthew 4)

FIRST PRELUDE –

Consider Jesus, led into the desert.

SECOND PRELUDE –

Pray that you may always be ready to resist the attacks of the evil one.

- Pause and Reflect -

FIRST POINT –

Each precise moment was known to the Eternal Father and pre-ordained from all eternity. Temptations, death, sickness, may come unawares to us. They come at the precise moment appointed by Eternal Wisdom and Unchangeable Love. Can we doubt, if we love God at all, that that moment is the best in which they could happen? How often do we hear people say, "If so-and-so had not died just then," or "If it had not happened just at such a moment." Oh! What unbelief, what mistrust we have in the tenderest of Hearts. Surely the moment of our bereavement or of our trial was precisely the moment when it was best, and wisest, and kindest for us. Let us then no longer complain of the appointments of our Heavenly Father, since Wisdom and Love combine to make all things work together for our eternal salvation;

and if we fail in a trial, let us at least acknowledge that God intended it for our greater merit, had we but corresponded with His designs.

Second Point –

Consider that, since we do not know the moment when death or temptation may come, we should endeavor to be always prepared for either. There are moments marked in our lives for special trial. We know not the day nor the hour, though we may well believe that we would be forewarned were it for our greater good; but if we are not warned, how necessary is constant watchfulness. Let us make it a special purpose during this holy season to watch for the least approach of danger. The vigilant will see and receive warnings which the thoughtless will pass unheeded.

Third Point –

Consider how we may console the Heart of Jesus at the moment of His temptation. Let us bend at His blessed Feet, or if we may, before the tabernacle where, for our love, He remains too often neglected and alone; and let us humbly, earnestly, pray that He will Himself offer for us to the Eternal Father the infinite merit of His vigilance, of His prompt and efficacious resistance of temptation, to obtain pardon for our past carelessness, and the graces we need for the future, that we may never be found unprepared in the moment of danger. Say a Hail Mary for this intention and for all who during this year may be tried by sudden and violent temptations.

Aspiration –

Heart of Jesus, resisting temptation victoriously, help me to resist in Your name and by Your power.

Saturday after Ash Wednesday

The Heart of Jesus, Tempted by the Devil

"Then was Jesus led by the Spirit into the desert to be tempted by the devil."

(Matthew 4)

FIRST PRELUDE –

Consider Jesus tempted by the devil, and enduring the presence of the evil one.

SECOND PRELUDE –

Pray that you may have a horror of sin and of the tempter's suggestions.

- Pause and Reflect -

FIRST POINT –

And must our Divine Lord stoop so low for our sakes? Must He contend, face to face, with the prince of darkness? Must He endure the loathsome presence of the fiend? Oh! Sin, how horrible you seem, while we contemplate the temptations in the lonely desert. One instantaneous manifestation of His Divinity, one glance of power, one word from His blessed lips, one secret wish of His adorable heart, and the demon would have fled forever to hell—but no, Jesus thinks of His children. He will experience what they must suffer; He will know to the utmost how they will be tried; and now no child of Adam can say, even in his most secret thoughts, "God knows not how I am tempted." He knows, He feels, He pities; and He has purchased grace for you to resist every temptation. "Because he himself was tested through what he suffered, he is able to help those who are being tested" (Hebrews 2:18).

SECOND POINT –

Consider the courage we ought to gain from this condescension of our Lord. Some persons, from natural timidity, and others from spiritual weakness, or from the effect by long habits of yielding to it, dread temptation so excessively that their lives are almost a martyrdom of fear. Their very dread becomes a source of temptation in itself, and deprives them of that generosity necessary for the attainment of great sanctity. Let them meditate on Jesus tempted by the devil, enduring the presence of the foul fiend, and for our sakes submitting to hear His suggestions. In this moment He purchases for us the grace to resist every possible temptation, and the courage to endure, should we be long and continually assaulted.

THIRD POINT –

Consider how we may console the Heart of Jesus, tempted by the devil. Let us offer the infinite merit of His victory to the Eternal Father, that we may have the grace to conquer, whenever and however we are tempted. Each soul thinks its own trial the hardest to bear, for each feels the constant pressure of its own burden while it is ignorant of that of others. But Jesus knows and understands the sufferings of every Child of Adam. In His Sacred and tempted Heart, let us seek our refuge, our strength, and our salvation. Say three Our Fathers for this intention, and offer them in union with all the efficacious resistance which the saints in Heaven have made to temptation, to console the Heart of Jesus tempted in the desert, and to help all the poor of this earth who may be tempted to commit sin.

ASPIRATION –

Heart of Jesus, victoriously resisting temptation, help me to conquer when tempted.

First Sunday of Lent

The Heart of Jesus, Fasting in the Desert

"He fasted for forty days and forty nights…"
(Matthew 4:2)

FIRST POINT –

The Bridegroom fasts, and shall the faithful bride refuse to suffer with Him? Is fasting necessary for Him, or is it so necessary and so painful for us that by His example, He must give us strength and courage? Jesus fasts, and shall we refuse to join Him? No, we will begin with fervor, and will do all in our power to imitate Him. We cannot follow His example, so as to remain altogether without food, but we will endeavour, as nearly as possible, to comply with all that the Church requires. It is His voice speaking to us, and telling us how we may best sympathize with His sufferings.

SECOND POINT –

Consider the infinite merit of the fast of Jesus. It has sanctified and given merit to every fast and abstinence which the faithful have since observed. We marvel as we read about the lives of the saints, how they lived for days and weeks, and even for several years, without the nourishment which is so necessary for human begins. Here is the secret of their strength: the fast of Jesus in the lonely desert obtained for them the grace to perform these acts of heroic virtue. They lived on the life of Christ, and we in our measure must strive to follow their example. He has obtained all the graces we need, and we require it, perhaps as much, to refrain from exceeding what is absolutely necessary to support our physical strength, while they macerate their bodies by a penance beyond our power of imitation. Let us, then, offer our Lent in union with His forty days of fasting; this will supply for our deficiencies, strengthen our weakness, and make the duty to which we are obliged a holocaust of love. Fasting will scarcely be a penance when we fast with Jesus.

THIRD POINT –

Consider how we may console the Heart of Jesus fasting in the desert. Let us endeavour this Lent to make up for the deficiencies of former years. Perhaps we have too often and too easily sought dispensations, but now, strengthened by the example of Jesus, we will strive to yield less often to nature. Our Divine Lord does not ask us to exceed our strength. He who accepts the cup of cold water from those who have no more to give, will likewise accept the abstinence of those who cannot fast, the little self-denials of those who cannot abstain if sickness forbids. But let us be most careful that we are not our judges in such matters. Our weak nature will complain and the tempter will be near; in obedience lies our security and our strength. Let us also perform three acts of mortification, and repeat the fifty-first psalm in reparation for those who, through human respect or self-love, break the fasts and abstinences of the Church; let us offer to the Eternal Father the infinite merit of the fast of Jesus, to obtain grace and strength for them, and for ourselves, that we may perform this holy duty with more courage.

ASPIRATION –

Heart of Jesus, fasting in the desert, give me the grace to imitate Your example.

Second Meditation
The Heart of Jesus, Tempted to Work a Miracle to Appease His Hunger

"The tempter approached and said to him, 'If you are the Son of God, command that these stones become loaves of bread.'"

(Matthew 4:3)

First Prelude –

Pray that you may be so enlightened with spiritual discernment that you may always discern the snares of the tempter.

- Pause and Reflect -

First Point –

Consider the artfulness of the evil one: "If you are the Son of God." Truly had it been any other than the Son of God, the tempter would have gained his point. Thus he approaches us; at first with cautious suggestions, with slight whispers, with vague suspicions, with trifling mistrusts. We are suffering spiritual trials of darkness and desolation, prayer has become a burden; faith seems to have quenched its lamp and charity to have extinguished its flame. "If you are a Christian," he says, "if you are the chosen spouse of Christ, ask to be delivered from tests and trials, ask that these stones be made bread that you may be refreshed, and if it be not done, believe that you are no longer in the favour and grace of God, and give up all for lost." Despair is the deadliest weapon of the foe, and he knows it.

Second Point –

Consider the answer of Jesus: He does not reveal His Divinity to the evil one. The Heart of Jesus knows only the deepest humility, and it is the humble who conquer best when in conflict with the powers of darkness. "It is written," replies our Divine Lord, "not in bread alone does man live, but in every word that proceeds from the mouth of God." Thus let us also reply to temptations to mistrust and despair. Appearances may be against the providences of God in our regard, either temporally or spiritually, but let us ever answer the tempter and our own faithless hearts with an "it is written." Are we in temporal need, and does our labour or our strength fail us so that we know not where tomorrow's bread can be procured? Or have we vowed poverty, and are we suffering some of the inconveniences of our state, perhaps only felt because of our mortification; or perhaps harder to bear if, from our former life, some of its comfort had become almost necessaries? Still "it is written: your Father knows that you have need of all these things." Your Father knows, is not that enough, O faithless heart? Bear your temptation bravely, and if your need is not supplied—if the stones remain stones—remember the Heart of Jesus hungry in the desert. No miracle is worked for His relief, and will you ask one for yours, when if you bear your trial courageously you will give such glory to God? But your temptation may be spiritual, you may have spent years endeavoring to conquer yourself, or resisting some constant importunate temptation; or your affections may have been wronged to the uttermost by bereavement or by the unkindness of others: again, "It is written: and you have forgotten the consolation which speaks to you as unto children, saying: 'My son, neglect not the discipline of the Lord: neither be wearied if you are rebuked by Him. For whom the Lord loves He chastises, and He scourges every person whom He receives'" (Hebrews 12:5–6).

Third Point –

Consider how you may console the Heart of Jesus, tempted in the desert. Offer His victory to the Eternal Father in reparation for your infidelities when under temptations, and to obtain grace and courage when you are exposed to such trials in the future.

Aspiration –

We therefore pray, Lord, that You help Your servants, whom You have redeemed with Your Precious Blood.

Second Sunday of Lent

The Heart of Jesus, Condescending to Accept the Service of Angels

"Then the devil left him and, behold, angels came and ministered to him."

(Matthew 4:11)

First Prelude –

Consider the Heart of Jesus, desiring and accepting consolation for our sake.

Second Prelude –

Pray that you may ever be ready to minister consolation to others.

- Pause and Reflect -

First Point –

Angels came and ministered to Him; are we ready to minister to others in their necessities? We do not speak now of deeds of heroic charity, or of temporal relief of the poor, or of the ordinary works of mercy; rather let us at present consider how we act towards those with whom we associate daily, when we see them suffering from depression or temptation. But we may make excuses, saying it is our business, our rule, or our occupations which prevent us from interfering with what does not concern us; or that our duty is with ourselves; besides, we might only make matters worse if we interfered. "Angels came and ministered to him"; and this for our example and our instruction, and are we to walk by on the other side in cold dignity or indifference, like the priest or the Levite?

SECOND POINT –

Consider how we may minister to others who experience temptation; how we can learn from the example of the angels ministering to Christ in the desert; a little charity, one little spark of heavenly love, would suggest a thousand ways. You see a person in trouble; some would be too much absorbed in themselves to notice it, and would say and do a hundred little things that would jar again and again on a wounded heart, but this will not be your case: you will make no curious inquires, you will break no rule, you will form no conjectures (unless indeed an office or position of superiority oblige you); you will not even wish to know what the trial is, whether mental or bodily; whether sorrow for sin, or struggle with temptation; but you will do all in your power by a gentle manner, by a kind, wisely-timed word, or even by a forbearing silence, to help and comfort this tempted soul. Let us consider how we have felt ourselves, when some little thoughtful kindness was shown us in a moment of depression or grief; and it will help us in our conduct towards others.

THIRD POINT –

Consider how you may console the Heart of Jesus for His humiliation in accepting consolation from His own creatures. Let it be so by the tenderest charity towards all who are in any affliction, from the poor half-starved wailing infant in your school or neighborhood, to the patient, much-tried superior or parent, who must have, at best, so many, and such anxious cares. If possible, let no day pass during this holy season without some act of thoughtful charity towards others. Say a Hail Mary for all who are in affliction and who are tried by the unkindness of others, offering this mystery to the Eternal Father for them; and in satisfaction for all the sins that may be committed during this year against charity.

ASPIRATION –

Heat of Jesus, Consoler of the afflicted, grant us the grace of special tenderness towards all who are in sorrow.

SECOND MEDITATION

Jesus has No Place to Lay His Head

"Foxes have dens and birds of the sky have nests, but the Son of Man has nowhere to rest his head."
(Matthew 8:20)

FIRST PRELUDE –

Consider your Divine Master, homeless and alone at evening.

SECOND PRELUDE –

Pray for the grace to imitate His poverty as far as your circumstances will permit.

- Pause and Reflect -

First Point –

Consider the words of our Divine Lord: "The foxes have holes, and the birds of the air have nests: but the Son of Man has nowhere to lay His head." Oh, my God, what poverty, what homelessness! We have a home, we have a place to lay our heads, however poor it may be; but Jesus Himself tells us that the foxes and the birds are better off than He is. His heart is too tender to let others suffer what He endures Himself. The foxes, the proud and rich ones of the earth, have their holes and shelter in them; they are warm, they are clothed, they have abundance; and the birds, the blessed ones who strive to sore aloft, to follow Jesus in spirit, to raise themselves above terrestrial things—they have their nests. True, these nests may be destroyed by a rough blast, or dashed to the ground by a rude blow; still, they have a shelter, and it is all they ask; for they would be like Jesus as far as may be, and some even can say when they lie down to rest at night, "Oh, my God, even the very pillow I use is not my own," for they have vowed poverty; still they have a shelter and a place of repose, a nest where they may rest in passing on their way to their Father's palaces. But Jesus has no rest.

Second Point –

Consider the words of the Holy Gospel according to Saint John: "Every man returned to his own house, and Jesus went to the Mount of Olives." He had been teaching, and healing, and comforting the ignorant and sick all day. He had done all He could for those around Him, and now what reward does He receive? Every man returns to his own house, but we do not hear that anyone invites Jesus to accompany him. He has no home, no place to rest in for the night; He goes to the Mount of Olives. There, in some cold cave, or perhaps on the damp grass, under the shade of the great olive trees, He spends the night in prayer. And the people to whom He has been so kind have gone home, and have made themselves comfortable at their firesides, and drawn their curtains close, and partaken of their evening meal, and enjoyed the smiles and caresses of those they loved. But Jesus has no home.

Third Point –

Consider how we may console the homeless Heart of Jesus. Oh, we may, we can console Him; thank God for it, or our hearts would break. He wants a home now, He is asking for it every day. He even begs us to give it to Him, and will we refuse? The hearts of His faithful ones are the nests where Jesus loves to dwell, the gardens where He gathers lilies. Oh, let us take Him home with us. He will put up with a great deal that no one else would bear with, if we will only receive Him into our house. He would not have a home on earth or a place to lay His blessed Head, that He might teach us to love poverty, and to practice detachment from the things of earth; but now His love to us is so excessive that He cannot rest away from us even in His own most glorious home. And He asks us to receive Him beneath our roof, and this under the form of Bread; lest if we beheld His Presence with bodily eyes we should tremble to entertain so glorious a guest.

Aspiration –

Oh most poor Jesus, teach me, for Your sake, to love and practice holy poverty.

The Third Sunday of Lent

The Heart of Jesus, Rising Very Early in the Morning

"Rising very early before dawn, he left and went off to a deserted place, where he prayed."

(Mark 1:35)

FIRST PRELUDE –

Consider your Divine Lord, going forth at early morning to a deserted place.

SECOND PRELUDE –

Pray for the grace to imitate His example as far as your circumstances in life will permit.

- Pause and Reflect -

FIRST POINT –

Consider the consolation that this action of our Divine Lord affords to all who are obliged by their rule, or by their circumstances in life, to rise early. Those who have spent the night in vanity or sin, are now seeking a fevered, restless sleep; what can this be but fresh sorrow to the Heart of Jesus? But you can console Him. Rising early may be the first act of mortification that you have to offer Him for the day; let it be done generously and cheerfully. If we rise only when we feel refreshed and rested, we only do what is done by those who have no rule but natural instinct, or by those who do not understand the value of self-sacrifice. But if we rise still weary from the labors of the previous day, or suffering from the indisposition we may have felt during the night, then we perform an act of mortification most acceptable to God. Alas for the religious who cannot sacrifice herself in this matter, who is asking for constant dispensations for the most trifling causes; when perhaps she can spend the day in active exertion in a duty, or even in an occupation of her own choosing, which pleases her Lord.

SECOND POINT –

Consider how many thousands are obliged to rise early to procure by their labor the commonest necessities of life. Oh, what sufferings the poor endure from want of rest and food; what merit and consolation would they have, if they were taught that by this, they might become like their Divine Lord; that by uniting their fatigues with His, they might merit rewards beyond all they could conceive or desire. Let us endeavour to instruct the poor on such matters, and thus participate in acts of virtue, and give increased glory to our Divine Master.

THIRD POINT –

Consider how we may console the Heart of Jesus, rising very early in the morning. Let it be by sacrificing ourselves in this matter as much as possible. To many persons it is the greatest act of mortification that the day affords; how desirable then that it should be generously offered to God. Perhaps on our fidelity to this duty many graces may depend. Jesus has obtained for us the grace we need; He asks of us only what He has Himself done.

Aspiration –

By Your lonely watching and Your midnight prayer, sweet Jesus, have mercy upon me.

Second Meditation

The Heart of Jesus, Weeping at the Tomb of Lazarus

"And Jesus wept."

(John 11:35)

First Prelude –

Consider Jesus at the tomb of Lazarus, moved to tears by the sorrow of Martha and Mary.

Second Prelude –

Pray for an ever-increasing tenderness towards those who are in sorrow.

- Pause and Reflect -

First Point –

"Jesus wept!" Oh, precious tears, that will serve to console all Christian mourners until mourning has forever ceased in the land where sorrow cannot come. The Jews see Jesus weeping, and even their hard hearts seem for a moment touched, and they exclaim, "Behold, how He loved him." A moment more, and their cruel, restless suspicions are aroused, and the Heart of Jesus is wronged again by their unbelief. "Could not He that opened the eyes of the man born blind, have caused that this man should not die?" Truly He could. But is it only the Jews who reproach Jesus? Have we never said in our secret thoughts, "Could not He have spared my sister or my brother, my father or my mother, my husband or my child?" Alas for the Heart of Jesus, whenever they who profess to believe in Him can mistrust His love. He is omnipotent, oh faithless soul, He could have caused that Lazarus should not die, but where then would have been the glorious miracle of his resurrection? And had He spared those for whom you mourn, can you tell what their future life might have been, or what glory God may receive, or what benefit may accrue to yourself from the trial which seems so hard to bear? Perhaps in your regard it will be the occasion of as great a miracle as the raising of Lazarus.

Second Point –

Consider how Jesus, by His tears, has hallowed our natural affections. Sanctity does not wither up the heart and deaden it to all interest in and love for others; rather does it so deepen our tenderness for those around us as to increase the trials of life, while it adds daily to their merit. Jesus wept at the tomb of Lazarus; the tenderness of the tenderest of human hearts was moved even to tears when He beheld the grief of those He loved. Saint John himself, who was so especially beloved to Our Divine Lord, tells us that "Jesus loved Martha, and her sister Mary, and Lazarus," and that when He saw Mary "weeping, and the Jews that came with her, He groaned in the spirit, and troubled Himself." Oh, sweet Jesus, weeping at the tomb of Lazarus, teach us how to love aright, how to give to others the deepest affection and the gentlest sympathy in their sorrow, and yet to love them only in You and for You. Oh, by Your tears, purify us from all that is merely human in our attachments, and sanctify that which You permit us to receive or to give.

THIRD POINT –

Consider how we may console the Heart of Jesus, weeping at the tomb of Lazarus. Let it be by endeavouring to become more like Him in our conduct towards others. Many persons hide a deep selfishness under the pretext of practicing perfection. They care not for the sorrows of and have no sympathy in the joys of others, and thus perhaps save themselves many an hour's grief, but do they please the Heart of Jesus? And many more lavish on earthly objects the love of ardent, tender hearts, forgetting that all affection, to be sanctified, must pass through the Heart of Jesus, that He may have its first freshness and its first favour. Nor will this lessen its value; rather will such affection be deepened a hundredfold, and carry with it a tenderness and power to soothe the afflicted far beyond that which is merely human.

ASPIRATION –

Heart of Jesus, pour into mine Your tenderness, and have mercy upon me.

Fourth Sunday of Lent

The Heart of Jesus, Weeping over Jerusalem

"As he drew near, he saw the city and wept over it, saying, 'If this day you only knew what makes for peace—but now it is hidden from your eyes.'"
(Luke 19:41–42)

FIRST PRELUDE –

Consider Jesus approaching the city of Jerusalem, the city chosen by God for His special worship, but now rejecting the very God in Whose temple daily sacrifice is offered.

SECOND PRELUDE –

Pray that you may be enlightened spiritually, that you may not be deprived of the graces necessary for salvation.

- Pause and Reflect -

FIRST POINT –

Jesus weeps over Jerusalem. "Three times," says Saint Bonaventure, "we are told that our Divine Lord wept." First at the tomb of Lazarus, where His tears were those of the tenderest sympathy for human misery; second as He approached Jerusalem, when He wept for the spiritual blindness of men; and third in His passion, when the Apostle Saint Paul tells us that "with a strong cry and tears, He offered up prayers and supplications." Who may tell what treasures of grace are purchased by these tears of Jesus? Jesus weeps, and can we expect to be spared from sorrow? His life is one of continual suffering, exterior and interior, and can we ask to live free from pain? The Heart of Jesus causes Him special sufferings because of the intensity of His love, and how keen are those sufferings caused by His affections. Let us learn to regulate our affections, to sanctify them by uniting them with the sufferings of the Heart of our Divine Lord. Let us console ourselves and others, if our daily cross is caused or increased by affection for others; by anxiety for their spiritual welfare, or even for their bodily health.

Second Point –

Jerusalem had killed the prophets, had stoned them that were sent unto her, and although our Divine Lord reproaches her with her guilt, He exclaims, "How often would I have gathered together your children, as the hen gathers her chicks under her wings, and you would not." Christian soul, have you never refused to shelter yourself under the wings of your Redeemer? Have you never refused to hear His call, kinder than that of the tenderest Mother? And if, happily, you have listened and are safe, is there no place even yet nearer to His Sacred Heart in which He calls you to nestle if you would hear His voice, and are there none wandering far from those blessed wings whom you might beckon beneath their shelter?

Third Point –

Consider what we can do to console the Heart of Jesus weeping over Jerusalem. These tears have not been shed in vain. Let us gather them up reverently and offer them one by one to the Eternal Father. A single tear could ransom a hundred worlds. Saint Augustine says that one tear shed out of the remembrance of the Passion of Jesus is better than a pilgrimage to Jerusalem, or a year fasting on bread and water. If our tears shed at the mere remembrance of the Passion of Jesus can be of such value, of what infinite value must be the tears shed by Jesus Himself. Consider how many thousands there are who never give even a passing thought to the Passion of Jesus. How many Fridays come and go, and people only remember it as a day of abstinence, and offer no reparation for the deadliest crime that human guilt could accomplish, and offer no acts of love to console the Heart of Him who has died from the excess of His love for us. Let us endeavour now to do what we can in this matter. Let us begin each Friday to think a little of the sufferings of our God, and to offer Him some acts of love and condolence, inducing others, as far as we can, to practice the same devotion.

ASPIRATION –

They that sow in tears shall reap in joy.

Second Meditation
The Heart of Jesus, Washing the Feet of His Disciples

"Then he poured water into a basin and began to wash the disciples' feet..."

(John 13:5)

First Prelude –

Consider the Creator of heaven and earth kneeling at the feet of His creatures and humbly washing them.

Second Prelude –

Pray for the grace to understand this mystery.

First Point –

When Jesus announced to His disciples the near approach of His Passion, and declared that He should be mocked and scourged and crucified, their first thought seems to have been who should succeed to His authority when He was taken from them. We do not hear that they uttered one word of sympathy, one expression of grief. Probably at that time they hardly understood His words, and still expected some temporal kingdom in which they should participate. And now, on the very night of His Passion, the strife is again renewed. He had already endeavoured to teach them humility. He told them it was only for the Gentiles, for those who knew not God, "to lord it" over others but for them, whosoever would be first should "be the servant of all." He adds, "For the Son of Man also is not come to be ministered to but to minister." His life had been one unceasing example of the deepest humility, and yet His own chosen ones had not learned the lesson. Now He has but just declared to them that the Son of Man shall be betrayed by one of them; for a few moments terror seizes them, and they inquire who it might be who shall do this dreadful deed. A moment more and the one uppermost thought is which of them should be greatest.

Second Point –

Consider the example of humility which Jesus gives them. His last act in His intercourse with others is to practice humility and to preach charity. He washes the feet of His disciples, and then He utters that sublime discourse which shall be the treasure of all faithful hearts to the end of time. Mediate, O Christian soul, as best you can, on the tenderness and love with which Jesus performs this menial service. Count up, as far as you may imagine them, the graces it has purchased for those who, in their measure, have imitated His example. No act of lowliness, performed by saintly souls, has obtained its merit but from union with the lowliness of Jesus. Consider further the unexampled patience of the Heart of Jesus. No mother has ever borne with a wayward, or a sinful child, with one half the tenderness that the God of Heaven has shown to His guilty creatures. There are no reproaches for their neglect of His often repeated instructions, no complaints of their forgetfulness of His approaching agony; no feeling, if we may say so reverently, for Himself, when He receives no sympathy from those who at such a time should have forgotten themselves, and overwhelmed Him with the deepest and most reverent tenderness. Once more He meekly instructs them: "The disciple is not greater than his Lord." Once more He tells them that they must not be as the Gentiles, to whom the very idea of humiliations is unknown; and then, as if He feared lest the lesson might be too hard for them, as if He longed to give them any consolation that He could, He speaks to them of His Father's Kingdom; He tells them of the greatness and the dignity they shall yet enjoy, and that they "shall eat and drink at His table," and "sit upon thrones, judging the twelve tribes of Israel." As if He would console them for present humilities by the hope of future glory. When shall we ever fathom the depth of tenderness of the Heart of Jesus? When shall we learn to imitate it in our intercourse with others? Who but Jesus would mingle consolation so skillfully with reproof? Who but Jesus would condescend so patiently to human weakness? He knows how hard it is for them to learn the lesson of humility. He waits for the best time and opportunity to teach them, and then He almost fears lest the lesson should be too much for them. He must correct, but there shall be all the sweetness and consolation in the correction that the Heart of God can devise.

THIRD POINT –

Consider how we may console the Heart of Jesus, washing the feet of His disciples. Let it be by endeavouring to instruct others by our example, as well as by our words. Example preaches a sermon that cannot be misunderstood. We may not even consciously notice the example of those around us, but any thoughtful mind will at once acknowledge that it has a deep influence on us. Thoughtless persons will perhaps be even more influenced than others by example, though they are less likely to perceive it. One saintly nun in a convent; one holy girl in a school; one pious workman in a shop; one good practical Catholic in a regiment or a police barrack; who may tell until the great day of reckoning what acts of virtue have been performed, what conversions effected through their example? And those whose position in life is higher, who therefore have greater influence, what may they not do for God, even by performing the most exalted duties of their state as good Christians? Offer to the Eternal Father the infinite merit of the example of Jesus in this mystery, to obtain for yourself the grace to give good example to others, and for all Catholics who are in a high position in this country, saying the Miserere Psalm (Psalm 51) in atonement for the scandal which has been given by the bad example of those who profess the Faith but do not practice it.

ASPIRATION -

Heart of Jesus, example of true humility, teach me to live like You.

The Fifth Sunday of Lent

The Heart of Jesus, Kneeling at the Feet of Peter

"What I am doing, you do not understand now, but you will understand later."

(John 13:7)

FIRST PRELUDE –

Consider your Divine Lord, kneeling at the feet of Saint Peter, and addressing to him these words.

SECOND PRELUDE –

Pray for the gift of faith and a trustful spirit.

- Pause and Reflect -

FIRST POINT –

Consider the words of our Divine Lord, "What I do, you know not now, but you shall know hereafter." Peter, the ardent, loving, impetuous disciple, shrinks back dismayed; as he beholds his Lord and Master at his feet, he cannot believe it possible that such an act of condescension should be exercised towards him. There is humility in his impetuosity, and there is that peculiar feeling, always so strong in those whose affections are ardent, which cannot bear even to witness the humiliation of their object. Once more let us admire the meekness of Jesus. How patiently He explains, how calmly He waits until His apostle will permit Him to accomplish the act of humility for which His Heart yearns. Truly what He "does we know not now." What intellect can understand, what depth of love, however saintly, can appreciate what Jesus does? Let us learn at least to trust Him: even to ourselves how often and how sweetly does He utter these very words: "What I do you know not now." This is the time of trial, the time when faith must be refined and purified, the time when obedience must be tried, and love must learn its deepest lessons amidst suffering and contempt. But the "hereafter" comes, it is very near. Then will the mourner understand why he was afflicted; the poor, why they were permitted to suffer poverty; the good, why their best and holiest plans were thwarted and destroyed. Then shall the just man know why the wicked prosper, and the oppressed understand why the exaction of his oppressor was permitted.

Second Point –

But it shall be singularly and especially those who have dedicated their lives to penance and humiliation, who shall "know hereafter" what Jesus does, and what He requires from them now. At best they have but faint glimpses of the deep value of suffering, of the treasure of poverty, of the nobleness of humiliation, of the saintliness of obedience, of the angelic nature of purity. They live by faith, and by faith, heroically practice heroic virtue. But as yet they understand not all they do, nor all that is done in their regard. Take only the virtue of humility, and imagine, if you can, what must be its excellence, its hidden depths of meaning, when we see in it the daily exercise of God. And yet who may tell all the treasures that it conceals—who may understand it sufficiently, to value it as it is valued by God?

Oh spouse of Christ, "you know not now, but you shall know hereafter." You shall know the value of your obedience, and the worth of your poverty; you shall understand why you were called to this life of penance, why interiorly urged to these constant little acts of self-mortification. In the light of that city whose gates are of pearl and whose foundation is precious stone, you shall read aright the pages of your history, and shall see that the most loving of providences watched over and ordered its every circumstance; that the tenderest of Hearts meted out and prepared its every trial. And you shall know hereafter the love of that Heart, you shall fathom the depth of its mysteries; and you shall lead in no doubtful fashion the life of the spouse on earth, and understand as far as finite capacity can, the hidden meanings of His every action; the deep wisdom of His every word; and know what He has done and purchased for His Church by the most trifling circumstances of His human life.

THIRD POINT -

Consider how we may console the Heart of Jesus washing the feet of Peter. Let it be by great reverence and respect towards our superiors. Behold Jesus Himself at the feet of His Vicar. Oh, what a lesson to teach us tender and respectful love towards him who sits in the Chair of Peter. Jesus goes first to Peter, and washes his feet. The priest must first be purified, and then he will be able to purify the flock committed to his charge; the priest must first be instructed, and then he will be able to teach the sheep of God.

ASPIRATION -

Heart of Jesus, most lowly, have mercy on me.

Second Meditation
The Heart of Jesus, Praying for Us Before His Passion

"I pray not only for them, but also for those who will believe in me through their word..."

(John 17:20)

First Prelude –

Consider the Son of God with His eyes lifted up to heaven, praying to His Eternal Father.

Second Prelude –

Pray that you may be worthy to obtain all that He asked for you in His prayer.

- Pause and Reflect -

First Point –

Consider what it is that Jesus prays for. He prays that the Father will glorify Him because His hour is come. And what is this glory for which Jesus asks, which He so earnestly desires? Is it not suffering and the cross? When this is endured, but not until then, He desires to be glorified with the glory which He had with the Father before the world was. And shall we desire any other glory upon earth save that of the cross and humiliation? Jesus prays for the unity of the

Church. "Holy Father, keep them in your name, whom you have given me: that they may be one, as we also are one." Let us meditate on the union of the Eternal Father and the Word Incarnate, and then consider how far we have endeavoured to promote unity of faith by our prayers, and unity of heart among those with whom we live, by our example. Jesus prays that we may be kept from the evil of the world. Are we then endeavouring to keep our garments white and unspotted? Are we endeavouring more and more to free ourselves from the example and influence and maxims of the world? Or do we court its favour, seek high places, and desire the applause of the multitude or of those worldly persons with whom we may be obliged to associate? Even in the cloister are we free from the influence of the world without? Do we forget its maxims, renounce its pride, and disregard its distinctions of rank and honor? How difficult it is for those who walk in the midst of the torrent to escape being borne away by it, and yet for the comfort of such Jesus says: "I pray not that you should keep them from the evil." Yes, the Eternal Father will hear the prayer of Jesus on your behalf, and will keep you from evil if you do not yourself willfully escape from His keeping. Jesus prays, "Father, I will that where I am, they also whom you have given me may be with me." Oh burning love of the Heart of Jesus! He not only dies for our salvation, but He prays that it may be secured, as though He could not enjoy His glory without the children of His heart!

Second Point –

Consider for whom He prays. It is for His apostles first that He pours forth such supplications of tenderness as never before were uttered on earth. We might desire, as we read the holy gospel, that we had been in that upper room when Jesus prayed; that we also might have shared in His intercession, but He anticipates our desires. He dies for us before we are born, and He prays for our salvation before we have committed sin: "And not for them only do I pray, but for them also who through their word shall believe in me." Christian soul, if you do believe in Jesus, Jesus has prayed for you. You may be weak and helpless, you may be unlearned and ignorant, it matters not; Jesus knew you long before your existence on earth, and Jesus prayed for you. You may have the charge of many souls; you may have important duties to perform; you may sink under the weight of many responsibilities. Fear not, Christian soul, Jesus foreknew it all, and He prayed for you.

THIRD POINT –

Consider how we may console the Heart of Jesus, praying for us on the night before His passion. Let it be by our earnest efforts to practice the lessons He then taught, by our ardent prayers for the unity of the Church, and by using every means in our power to promote the conversion of those who are still wandering from the true fold. How many are there who linger on the threshold of the door that leads to its rich pastures, and yet fear, or hesitate, to enter. What if your prayers should obtain the grace of conversion for even one soul? Remember the words of Jesus: "I pray for them."

ASPIRATION -

Let peace be your strength, and abundance in your towers.

Some things to ponder:
In the liturgical calendar of the Church, Lent is an intense time of preparation for the great feast of Easter. It is an intense period because it is when we reflect, in an interior way, on how

we are living the Christian message. Each of us can ask ourselves: what type of person am I becoming? What areas in my life do I need to improve upon? What do I need to work on in my spiritual life? Prayer, fasting, and almsgiving are three means to help us enter into the Lenten Season in a reflective way, and to guide us on our interior journey with Christ.

In her meditations, Margaret Anna Cusack helps us to enter deeply into the season as she emphasizes the three areas for us to work on during Lent: prayer, fasting, and works of charity and service. She begins with Jesus being tempted in the desert. For forty days He is there, alone, at prayer, without food, and vulnerable to the temptations that may come His way. Margaret Anna wants us to enter that desert with the Lord. We all have the desert experiences of our lives, where we feel alone, hungry, and tempted; where we must rely totally on Jesus, so that we can overcome our temptations and take advantage of the opportunities Lent provides to help us become better people. Cusack's emphasis on prayer helps us to center ourselves on Christ.

Ask yourself:
This Lent, what am I looking to do to help improve my spiritual life? How can I be more prayerful? What loving acts of kindness can I perform for others this Lent? Where is God calling me to grow in my life right now?

Let us pray:
God of infinite mercy, grant that we who know your pity may rejoice in your forgiveness and gladly forgive others for the sake of Jesus Christ our Savior.
God our light,
Make your church like a rainbow shining and proclaiming to all the world that the storm is at an end, there is peace for those who seek it and love for the forgiving.
Merciful God,

*Grant to your faithful people pardon and peace, that we may be cleansed from all our sins and serve you with a quiet mind, through Jesus Christ our Redeemer.
Amen.*

(A New Zealand Prayer Book)

Holy Week

Palm Sunday

The Heart of Jesus, Clothed in a White Garment and Mocked by Herod

"Herod and his soldiers treated him contemptuously and mocked him, and after clothing him in resplendent garb, he sent him back to Pilate."

(Luke 23:11)

FIRST PRELUDE –

Consider Jesus standing in calm silence before the wicked King Herod.

SECOND PRELUDE –

Pray for the grace to imitate the meekness and wisdom of Jesus.

- Pause and Reflect -

FIRST POINT –

Consider the conduct of our Divine Lord before Herod. "Herod questioned Him in many words. But He answered him nothing." Jesus had never before refused to reply to those who questioned Him. The priests in the temple, the poor beggar by the wayside, the rich young man, and the little innocent child; none had been passed by without notice, but now, "Jesus answers nothing." The questions are asked, not in humble faith, but in insolent mockery. Herod desires to see a miracle, not that a wavering faith may be confirmed, but to gratify proud and idle curiosity. Herod is in the presence of Jesus, and yet he remains ignorant of His power, he cannot even hear His voice. How many are there who, like Herod, are near Jesus in bodily presence, but far from Him in spirit. How many in the hours of prayer and meditation hear not the voice of Jesus because their pride, or their willful distractions, or their habitual lack of mortification has deafened their spiritual healing. How many deprive themselves of graces, far more valuable to them than miracles, because they are not prepared to receive them by humility and self-sacrifice.

Second Point –

Consider the Eternal Wisdom of the Father, mocked and treated as a fool. He speaks no word, He works no miracle, and Herod, to revenge himself on Jesus, or because he really believes He is simple as He appears to be, clothes Him in a white garment of derision, and with "his army sets Him at naught." Oh my God, when they shall see You coming with thousands of angels in clouds of glory to judge the world, how terrible will be their fear. How many like Herod mock Jesus in the person of His priests. How many, like Herod and Pilate, who have formerly been at enmity with each other, become friends that they may persecute the Church of God. Today the Church celebrates the triumphal entry of Jesus into Jerusalem. It is true He comes meek and lowly, and riding upon a donkey, for His humility will bear no greater exaltation; but how is the scene charged in a few short days! Jesus walks the street of Jerusalem amidst the fears and mockeries of the people, clothed in garments of derision, sent from one tribunal to another as the sport of heathen judges. Truly is He "filled with reproaches," and made "a derision to His people."

THIRD POINT –

Consider how we may console the Heart of Jesus, clothed in a white garment and mocked by Herod. Why does Jesus suffer these outrages? Why does He not confound the impious King with a word, with a look? Why does He not declare Himself innocent, and prove it by a miracle? Because He not only desires to be condemned to death for our love, but He would teach us by His example one of the most difficult lessons which He requires us to practice. Had we not the force of His example, could we ever have learned to treat false accusations in silence? As it is, even though we have meditated on the silence of Jesus before His judges, even though we desire with our whole heart to imitate His example, even though we resolve most fervently to put a bridle upon our tongues, how frequently we fail. The word of excuse, if not of angry denial of our fault, rises quickly to our lips. It is uttered almost before we are conscious of it. To defend ourselves when blamed, whether justly or unjustly, seems less a matter of reflection than of instinct. But is it not precisely because it is so difficult that Jesus has submitted to these insults? Is it not because the victory costs us so much, that the reward will be so great? Oh then let us seek to console our Divine Lord by endeavouring to imitate His example. He is dumb as a lamb before his shearer and opens not His mouth. Let us consider also how false the judgments of the world are. Like Herod, it knows not truth when it hears it, and discerns not sanctity, even when nearest to it. But the consecrated spouse of Christ, and the soul that would practice perfection generously, has more to do than to submit in silence. She must rejoice to be accused, falsely or truly; and endeavour not only to be silent, offering no words of excuse, but even to control the excuses which her own imperfect thoughts too quickly suggest.

ASPIRATION -

Heart of Jesus, silent as a lamb before your accusers, grant me the grace to bear all accusations, whether great or trifling, whether false or true, without reply.

Monday in Holy Week

The Heart of Jesus, Scourged at the Pillar

"Therefore I shall have him flogged and then release him."
(Luke 23:16)

FIRST PRELUDE –

Consider the eagerness with which the cruel soldiers dragged Jesus away that they might scourge Him.

SECOND PRELUDE –

Pray for the grace to profit by, and to understand, what Jesus has suffered in this mystery.

- Pause and Reflect -

FIRST POINT –

Both Herod and Pilate have declared that Jesus is guiltless, and yet the Roman Governor proposes to chastise Him. He is in a great difficulty and wishes, if he can, to satisfy his conscience, and his unruly people. He will give a little to both. The guiltless one must suffer, because he has not courage to act on his convictions. Oh most iniquitous sentence! Who ever heard of a judge proposing to inflict punishment on a person whose innocence he loudly proclaimed? The most unreasonable, the cruelest of tyrants, have found some excuse, whether just or unjust, for their barbarities; but it remains for Jesus only to be declared guiltless, and still punished. We abhor the temporizing conduct of Pilate, but are we never guilty of such injustice ourselves? He does not believe Jesus to be God; he only imagines Him a good and innocent man; and when we say also to excuse ourselves, "It is not a mortal sin," or "It is only a trifle," and we please ourselves, or the world, and sacrifice Jesus, are we then less guilty than the Roman Governor?

SECOND POINT –

Consider the cruelty of the punishment inflicted on Jesus. Let us consider for a moment if we could bear to see any one we loved scourged to death; and yet we are told that if Jesus had not been God, He would have died under the lash of the soldiers. Oh, how His exquisitely delicate flesh must have quivered again and again, as blow after blow came upon it, inflicted with all the strength of barbarous hands, and all the cruelty of inhuman hearts. A Roman scourging was, of all punishments, the most fearful. The Jews were forbidden to give more than forty stripes to any one whom it might be necessary to chastise; but Jesus spares not Himself, though He will not permit others to suffer. Consider also the degradation of the punishment. It was reserved for slaves. We had become the slaves of sin, and Jesus suffered the punishment of slaves that we may be freed. But what slave ever suffered like Jesus? He had forbidden the Jews to exceed the number of forty stripes: "Lest your brother depart shamefully torn before your eyes." (Deuteronomy 25:3) But, oh, Christian soul, consider how your Brother Jesus departed from the hall where He was scourged. The most beautiful of the Sons of Men has now "no comeliness." He is "despised and the object of men," for "the chastisement of our peace is upon Him, and by His bruises we are healed" (Isaiah 53:5). His Sacred Body is one mass of wounds, and His garments are deluged with Blood.

THIRD POINT –

Consider how you may console the Heart of Jesus, scourged at the pillar. Who would refuse anything He asked them at such a moment? Oh if you will only endeavour to comfort Him, He who foreknew and foresaw all things will accept what you offer Him now, as if it had been given Him in the midst of His torments to close and heal one of His gaping wounds. It is supposed that Jesus suffered this cruel torture especially in atonement for sins of sensuality. Endeavour, then, to mortify your flesh in every possible way. Deny it ease, and rest, and gratification in food, in little things; you cannot, and perhaps ought not, to practice great corporal austerities, but He Who will reward even the cup of water given in His name will reward and accept with the tenderest love even such trifles as restraining the eyes from an unnecessary glance; denying our appetites some trifling gratification; or refusing our bodies an easier position.

ASPIRATION -

We therefore pray that You help Your servants, whom You have redeemed with Your Precious Blood.

Tuesday in Holy Week

The Heart of Jesus, Crowned with Thorns

"Then the soldiers of the governor took Jesus inside the praetorium and gathered the whole cohort around him. They stripped off his clothes and threw a scarlet military cloak about him. Weaving a crown out of thorns, they placed it on his head, and a reed in his right hand. And kneeling before him, they mocked him, saying, 'Hail, King of the Jews!' They spat upon him and took the reed and kept striking him on the head."

(Matthew 27:27–30)

FIRST PRELUDE –

Consider Jesus, crowned with the cruel crown of His espousals.

SECOND PRELUDE –

Pray that you may never drive the thorns deeper into His Sacred Head.

- Pause and Reflect -

FIRST POINT –

"They gathered together unto Him the whole band." It was a morning's sport for the Roman soldiers, and none would willingly be absent. Each has some fresh cruelty to suggest, or to practice, upon their unresisting victim. It is the day of His Espousals, the day of the joy of His Heart.

Oh, my God, what an espousal, what a joy! It is the Jewish synagogue, who has prepared for Him this cruel crown; well would it be if His spouses do not help to drive its sharp thorns deeper into His Sacred Head.

SECOND POINT –

Jesus offers no resistance. They may do with Him what they will. The garments, saturated with the blood of the scourging, are rudely torn from Him, and once more He bears the bitter shame of being exposed almost naked to a licentious rabble. The wounds are opened afresh, and His Blessed Frame thrills with agony, and trembles with weakness. But a cruel jeer, and a fresh insult, is the only notice taken of His sufferings. Oh, how royal You are in Your sorrows, my God, and My Lord. None ever approached You in greatness, as none could ever conceive the love with which You bear them. It was the custom among the Jews for the bridegroom to wear a crown; Jesus is about to espouse His Church, His crown till death. It is the day of the joy of His Heart. Oh, my God, my Savior! What strange joy is this that thrills Your blessed Heart? You are alone amidst Your tortures, and every moment they find some new insult for You. Now Your glorious countenance is defiled with shameful spitting, and now the agony which Your crown of thorns has caused is increased beyond all powers of endurance save Your own, by cruel blows which drive the thorns still deeper into Your quivering brain. Oh, my Jesus, what is this joy that makes this day so welcome to You? He thinks of His redeemed ones. He thinks of those who will sympathize in His sorrows, few though their number may be. He thinks of the day which He has purchased by His crown of thorns, and the little love He hopes to receive in return for His bitter suffering is the poor consolation in which He rejoices. Oh, spouse of Jesus crowned with thorns, will you not love Him?

Will you not endeavour to kindle the flame of His love in all hearts, at least by your fervent prayers?

THIRD POINT –

Consider how we may console the Heart of Jesus crowned with thorns. It is believed that our Divine Lord suffered this cruel torture to expiate what we call "little sins." How careful, then, should they be, who desire to console Him, to avoid even the least appearance of evil; who would willingly take even the smallest of those thorns and drive them into the Sacred Head of Jesus? Let us examine ourselves carefully and endeavour to purify our souls more and more, now that we are approaching nearer to the consummation of that awful mystery of the sacrifice of a God. Are there no little faults that we could correct, no little imperfections that we could be more earnest in avoiding?

ASPIRATION -

Heart of Jesus crowned with thorns, I adore You, and I love You.

Wednesday in Holy Week

The Heart of Jesus, carrying His Cross to Calvary

"So they took Jesus, and carrying the cross himself he went out to what is called the Place of the Skull, in Hebrew, Golgotha."

(John 17:16–17)

FIRST PRELUDE –

Consider the love with which Jesus endeavours to lift the ponderous Cross.

SECOND PRELUDE –

Pray for the grace to courageously, and cheerfully, bear whatever crosses the providence of God may ordain for you.

- Pause and Reflect -

FIRST POINT –

It is the last walk which Jesus takes on earth. Already His exhaustion has been so great, His sufferings so agonizing, that they truly needed the power of His Divinity to support them all: but He has more yet to do and to suffer for guilty man; the love of His Heart is not satisfied, and He permits His executioner to increase His torments. Let us endeavour reverently to contemplate the Heart of Jesus bearing this heavy load. The material weight of the Cross must have been immense; we may well believe that to support it on

His wounded and bleeding shoulders was not the least of His physical sufferings, but Jesus was to bear more than the material load beneath which He threatens to fall at every step. In that hour He bears every cross that has ever been, or ever will be, born by human hearts. The trials of bereavement, the pangs of separation, the interior sufferings, the awful temptations, the struggles with sin, the pains for want and hunger, the loss of rest, the days of weary toil, the little trials and vexations of domestic life, the heroic sacrifices of the saints, the daily strife of the less perfect; all that human misery has suffered, and human malice inflicted; all is borne in that hour by Jesus on His road to Calvary.

Second Point –

Jesus falls beneath His cross. He could have carried it to Calvary. His Divinity could have enabled Him to endure this trial in addition to those He had already born; thousands of angels were waiting for permission to raise that cruel burden from His blessed shoulders; but Jesus bears it until nature can support it no longer, and then He falls. It is for our love that He adds this to His sufferings. He knew the encouragement and the support that it would give us, when we sink beneath our trials. We are raised by His example, by the kind sympathy of our spiritual directors and superiors; but Jesus is unduly dragged from the ground by rough and cruel hands, and driven forward on His path of sorrow by inhuman blows. And where is Jesus going? No, not to a place of rest where His wounds may be cured, and His agonized Heart consoled. No: it is to Calvary that Jesus bears His cross. He carries it until He reaches the place where He must die. For though the material cross is placed on the shoulders of another, the Cross of our iniquities and our sorrows lies not the less heavily upon the Heart of Jesus.

Third Point –

Consider how we may console the Heart of Jesus, carrying His cross to Calvary. Let it be by our earnest endeavour to bear cheerfully whatever trials the providence of God may appoint for our sanctification. Our Heavenly Father will not try us more than He has tried His only Son. Will He not "give us all things" who has not even spared for us His own Son? (Romans 8:32). Jesus has obtained for us the strength to bear our cross, however heavy it may be. Only let us have courage, only let us seek to bear it to Calvary. Jesus carries His cross until death and dies upon it, and can we ask, or would we wish to be exempt from suffering? Are not they the most happy and the most privileged who, like Jesus, suffer all their lives, and die still upon the Cross?

Aspiration –

Heart of Jesus, bearing Your Cross to Calvary, help me to bear mine with love and generosity.

Holy Thursday

The Heart of Jesus, Nailed to the Cross

"They have pierced my hands and my feet
I can count all my bones.
They stare at me and gloat;
they divide my garments among them;
for my clothing they cast lots."

(Psalm 22:17–19)

FIRST PRELUDE –

Consider the love with which Jesus stretches forth His hands, that they may be pierced for us.

SECOND PRELUDE –

Pray for the grace to live a crucified life.

- Pause and Reflect -

FIRST POINT –

Until now, only the hands and feet of Jesus were exempt from cruel torture. "His Head is wounded with cruel thorns," says Saint Bernard, "that our wills may not be wounded by sin. His eyes are covered with the shadow of death that our eyes may be turned away from vanity. His ears, which in Heaven had heard only the Eternal Sanctus of the Angels, are deafened with shouts of 'Crucify Him, Crucify Him', that our ears may never be closed to the cries of the poor and may be turned away from all unholy sounds. His lips which have instructed angels and taught mankind, are deluged with vinegar and gall, that our lips may be enabled to utter truth, and to confess the Lord Our God." And now it only remains that His hands and His feet should share the wounds of His Blessed Body. Oh how freely, how generously He stretches out His blessed hands. Those hands, which have created the heavens; those hands which have healed the sick; those hands which have blessed the little ones, oh, how cruelly are they torn by those cruel nails!

Second Point –

Why is it that Jesus is nailed to the Cross? Surely there must be some deep lesson for us in this new torture. Is it that He would teach us how we should accept our crosses? Is it that He might teach us that the Cross must wound? How often we express ourselves as willing to suffer, even anxious for, and desirous for suffering; and the moment we feel the wound, we complain and ask eagerly for some alleviation of our pain. There can be no crucifixion without wounds. Suffering ceases to be suffering the moment that it ceases to give pain. Oh, let us love and pray to be wounded with Jesus. The soul consecrated to Christ is bound to have the marks of the nails. We envy those who have been marked with the visible Stigmata of the Lord Jesus. But every Spouse of Jesus Crucified is bound to bear the same Stigmata invisibly imprinted on her. Her vow of obedience, if truly kept, may be an ever-open wound. She must at every moment be ready to renounce her inclinations, to obey promptly every call, either of her rule or her superior; how many precious wounds will that soul receive during the day, which is bent on practicing perfection. How anxious will she be lest the least self-gratification should induce her to seek, or prefer any employment, lest she should become blinded to her own self-love, and therefore be indulged by her superior in what would be forbidden to others, because she is found to be too weak, or too imperfect, to bear some trifling contradiction. How will she rejoice if she feels the wound of the nail of poverty, in the denial of some little comfort in food or raiment. How will she rejoice if the nail of chastity wound her sensual inclination, and if the struggle to be all for God cost her many a weary conflict. O happy Spouse who bears the marks of her wounds, who knows that she must be wounded if she would be like her Lord, and who desires nothing but to be crucified with Jesus on Calvary.

THIRD POINT –

Consider how we may console the Heart of Jesus, nailed to the Cross on Calvary. It is for us that He endures this cruel torment, and we can best console Him by endeavouring to profit by what He has suffered. Whatever our trials in life may be, let us endeavour to unite them with the infinite merit of His. Let us try to support them patiently, even as He patiently submitted to the cruelty of the cruel men who pierced His blessed hands. Let us kneel beneath His cross and ask Him to bless us with those outstretched, bleeding Hands. For three long hours He hangs suspended by them. Will He ask us to bear as agonizing a suffering for as long a time? "And I," He says, "If I be lifted up from the earth, will draw all things to myself" (John 12:32). Oh sweet Jesus, draw us, for we long to be united to You; and if need be, oh nail us, dear Lord, to Your Cross, that our fickle, sinful wills may never be able to draw us away from You.

ASPIRATION –

We adore You O Christ and we bless You, because by Your holy cross You have redeemed the world.

Good Friday

The Heart of Jesus, Pierced with a Spear

"...but one soldier thrust his lance into his side, and immediately blood and water flowed out."

(John 19:34)

FIRST PRELUDE –

Consider Jesus hanging lifeless upon the Cross.

SECOND PRELUDE –

Pray for the grace to never wound the Heart of your Divine Lord.

- Pause and Reflect -

FIRST POINT –

Jesus hangs lifeless on the Cross. The darkness which veiled the day during His dying moments is gradually passing away. His enemies recover their courage, and His Mother's heart trembles with fresh anguish. He looks as if there were no blood left in His Body now, so pale has it become from the tree of the Cross; four streams have flowed for three long hours to water the paradise of the redeemed. But now these Precious Foundations have almost ceased to run. Jesus has spent three-and-thirty years in the work of our redemption. "Here," says Saint Bonaventure, "we should say that we had been created without difficulty." The wounds with which He was wounded in the house of those that loved Him testify to how great His suffering and His love have been. But the Heart of Jesus is not yet satisfied. There is still a little blood which He has not shed, and He wills to pour it forth to the last drop for our redemption. The Paschal Lamb was sacrificed; it remained but that the blood should be poured forth upon the door-posts, so that the destroying angel could no longer touch the people of God. Truly, having loved His own, He loves them unto the end.

Second Point –

"Immediately there came out blood and water." Eve is formed from the side of Adam while he lies unconscious in sleep. Jesus will have His Bride also come forth from His side, while He lies in the still sleep of death. So anxious is He to win her love that He will leave nothing undone that can touch her heart. He knows how often the hearts of His beloved ones will be pierced with acute sorrow. He knows the cruel pangs of bereavement—the keen sorrow that strong affection will constantly force through the very inmost of the soul, and He would provide a refuge and a remedy for the tried and tempted. Even they who, like Christ, are, as it were, hung between heaven and earth, separated from the world by their vows and from their celestial home by the chains of mortality; even they, who are thus crucified like their Lord, will often be, like Him, pierced with a spear of deepest sorrow. Blood and water will seem to flow forth from them also. Their affections will be tried even to the very quick, and their sufferings will often increase with their increasing sanctity. Oh, happy souls, whether in the cloister or the world, who live not only crucified, and hung between heaven and earth, but also transfixed with a sword of anguish.

Third Point –

Consider how we may console the Heart of Jesus, pierced with a spear. Today He says to us from the Cross, "Oh, my people what have I done to you, or in what have I afflicted you? What more ought I to do for you, and have not done it?" Let each one answer for themselves. Is there anything that Jesus could do for us which He has not done? What have we done for Him in return? Oh, let us endeavour to fly from those sins which have caused the death of our God. Let us endeavour to make reparation for the past and to form strong resolves for the future. What can we do on such a day as this but mourn for our Beloved Spouse, and offer sacrifices of propitiation, that God may mercifully absolve us from our sin and direct our inconsistent hearts?

Holy Saturday

The Heart of Jesus, Laid in the Tomb

"When it was evening, there came a rich man from Arimathea named Joseph, who was himself a disciple of Jesus… Taking the body, Joseph wrapped it [in] clean linen and laid it in his new tomb that he had hewn in the rock."
(Matthew 27:57, 59–60)

First Prelude –

Consider the Body of Jesus, laid in the silent grave.

Second Prelude –

Pray for the grace of a happy and glorious resurrection.

- Pause and Reflect -

First Point –

The worst that man's cruelty can do has been done to Jesus, and now His Mother, and a favoured few, are permitted to take Him from His Cross, and lay Him in the silent tomb. It is evening. The night is just closing in, and so with anxious haste they prepare to do Him the last services of love. Jesus would not descend from the Cross Himself, but when He can suffer no more He permits others to take Him down. It is as though He were jealous of every moment of pain, for each moment purchases infinite treasures for the children of His Heart. Slowly, and with difficulty, the nails are withdrawn from His wounded hands and feet, and He is laid once more in His Mother's arms. Oh, what agony must have wrung her blessed heart! How well she remembered the time when she had first taken Him in her arms—so beautiful, so gentle an Infant; and now, there is only a dead corpse, wounded, bruised, and emaciated, almost past recognition! Oh how terrible must sin have appeared to Mary in that hour, as she thought of what the Infant Child had been, and compared it with what the Dead Christ now was! But Mary had no other will than the will of Him who lay lifeless and helpless in her arms. He had willed to suffer for sin, and she also willed that He should suffer, and now, without a thought of self, she only considers how her own anguish may become a part of the Church's treasure; and she offers it to obtain grace and consolation for all Christian mourners to the end of time, to obtain for them the strength they need, and the resignation they have, when those whom they have loved and treasured lie cold and still in death.

Second Point –

Consider the exceeding love of Jesus in submitting to the humiliation of being laid in the grave. He might have glorified His Body instantly, and taken it triumphantly to heaven. He might have made all mankind witnesses of a glorious resurrection, but He desired to console mourners, and comfort those who fear the shadow of death and the darkness of the grave. He would teach us also the virtue of the hidden life. "That which you sow is not quickened except it dies first" (1 Corinthians 15:36). Death is the precursor of life, and the deeper the death, the more glorious will be the resurrection. Oh let us watch in spirit by the grave of Jesus, and weep there! Let us mourn for Him as for an only son, for the blameless Lord is slain. Jesus has died for us; let us also die with Him—die to ourselves, die to earthly anxieties and cares, and above all, die to the sins which have slain our dearest Lord.

Third Point –

Consider how we may console the Heart of Jesus, laid in the tomb. Let us endeavour to imitate the purity and humility of Jesus. He is born in a stable by the wayside, He is buried in the tomb of another, and even before His death, His very garments are taken from Him. He dies without a single possession, and He is buried by the charity of the few friends who still cling to Him. Was poverty ever so complete, or so perfectly practiced? Let us offer to the Eternal Father the poverty and burial of Jesus for all who have died, or who may die during the course of this year, and obtain for ourselves the grace of a happy death.

Aspiration -

From the depths I have cried to you, O Lord: Lord, hear my voice.

Some things to ponder:
In her meditations for Holy Week, Margaret Anna Cusack presents us with Jesus' trial, Passion, and death, and on Holy Saturday we see Jesus placed in the tomb as if in defeat. We pause for a moment to reflect on these mysteries, before turning to His triumphant conquering of death, that is, His Resurrection.

In her meditations, Margaret Anna Cusack encourages us in our prayer and reflections to comfort Jesus as we enter into His trial, suffering, and death. This comforting of our Lord can atone for our own sinfulness. Margaret Anna reminds us of our sinfulness, and directs us to correct our own faults since the sins of humanity have led Jesus to the sacrifice of the Cross. As this penitential season comes to a close, she directs our attention to this change of heart within us, which only the Passion and death of Jesus can lead to; and helps us draw closer to Him.

Finally, Margaret Anna Cusack reminds us that Jesus' trial, passion, and death give us the encouragement to bear our own trials in life, and help us to endure what may come our way in terms of suffering. Margaret Anna is such an encouraging example to us of someone who had to endure such trial and suffering in her own life. She knew the pain of the cross through her own challenges with health issues, as well as with being misunderstood and accused of wrongdoing. She was turned away by many in her church. She experienced isolation and loneliness. The pain of her parents' deaths, and the death of her fiancé, deeply wounded her heart. One might say that a good portion of her life was a kind of "Holy Week": Trial, Passion, and Death.

We can ask ourselves: what trials and sufferings have we undergone? How can we see these sufferings in light of Jesus' own suffering and death? Look back over the meditations for Holy Week, and find a phrase or image that Margaret Anna presents. Take time to reflect on it. Enter into your prayer for this Holy Week.

> Let us pray:
> *Almighty God, whose most dear Son went up to joy but first He suffered pain, and entered not into glory before He was crucified: Mercifully grant that we, walking in the way of the cross, may find it none other than the way of life and peace, through the same Son, Jesus Christ our Lord, who lives and reigns with you and the Holy Spirit, one God, forever and ever.*
> Amen.
> *(from the Book of Common Prayer)*

Easter Sunday, Easter Week, and Trinity Sunday

Easter Sunday

The Heart of Jesus Rising from the Tomb

"Jesus [said], 'I am the resurrection and the life.'"
(John 11:25)

FIRST PRELUDE –

Consider the sepulcher, now no longer sealed; the guards overthrown in terror and dismay, and the sweet Heart of Jesus rising glorious and triumphant.

SECOND PRELUDE –

Pray that, by His strength, and in the power of His grace, you may also rise triumphantly over sin in this world, and obtain a glorious resurrection in the life to come.

- Pause and Reflect -

FIRST POINT –

Consider the grave where Jesus lay. A moment before the midnight hour a body lay therein; a human heart, once full of life, but now cold and inanimate; a face pale and ghastly with the hues of death and the stains of blood, calm in its majestic sorrow and yet oh, how sorrowful! A wasted frame—wasted with three and thirty years of hourly suffering, worn by the cruel wrongs of creatures who were loved so much, and who loved so little. Oh, let us give one glance of burning love and one tear of heartfelt sorrow to our dead Jesus. We turn from meditations on His sufferings to enraptured contemplations of His rising, and, amid our Easter joys, let us remember, at least for a brief moment, how dearly they have been purchased for us!

Second Point –

But the midnight hour is heard. Jesus was born at midnight; at midnight He will come to judge the world; at midnight He rises gloriously, a conqueror from the tomb. He is the Resurrection, therefore He needs no power save His own to resuscitate His Humanity. Oh, let us shout to Him with shouts of joy: Alleluia! Alleluia! The courts of heaven are ringing with His praises, Alleluia! Alleluia! The Church on earth has scarcely words to express her joy, for how can the joy of the bride be fully expressed? O Jesus, our life, our love, we have no words to tell our gladness. You have risen! The winter of suffering is past, the springtime of sorrow is over, the autumn fruits are gathered in. Alleluia! Alleluia! You cannot suffer anymore, and if this thought alone has enabled us to bear close and constant contemplation of Your sufferings, how shall we not have joy within when we meditate on Your Resurrection's glory!

Third Point –

Consider how we may best worship and glorify the risen Heart of Jesus. 1. Let us run with the Holy Women to His tomb. There we may contemplate His wonders and adore His power; there we may offer our most fervent congratulations on His joyful resurrection. 2. Let us return with the women to declare what we have seen; let us tell "the brethren" of His risen love; let us manifest to all that His resurrection is also ours, and invite all to share in it by our words and our example. 3. Let us also rise with Him. We have sought, during the past season of penance, to die with Him; now let us rise again. He is the Resurrection and the Life, and when we receive Him into our hearts today, in that adorable Sacrament, of which He has said Himself: "He that feeds upon me, shall live by me," let us implore Him, by the love of His risen Heart, to give us life—life that becomes more strong and vigorous every day and hour until it becomes immortal.

ASPIRATION -

Sweet Heart of my Risen Jesus, may I rise with You!

Form your resolution, and place it in the Heart of Jesus Glorified.

Easter Monday

The Heart of Jesus, Manifesting Itself to Peter

First Prelude –

Peter was one of the first to visit the sepulcher. Even when the rest of the Apostles considered the words of the women to be idle tales, he "rose up and ran to the sepulcher." Thus does our sweet Jesus reward His faithful ones. They may fall, but they repent quickly. Their love may need many a trial before it becomes perfected, but still they love. Their faith may waver for a moment in times of trial and desolation, but soon it burns brighter and stronger than before. They love, and sweet Jesus only asks for love. He will bear with many faults for the sake of a little love. Oh, why are we so cold, why so slow to give what will cost us nothing, and what our risen Jesus desires so much? Better to be impetuous, better even to be unwise in our love, than not to love at all. Had Peter stayed at home to consider whether the words of the women were true or false—had he hesitated and doubted instead of running to the sepulcher—perhaps he would not have been vouchsafed this special visit of his risen Lord.

First Point –

Let us consider the words of the Holy Gospel: "He appeared to Simon." Yes, it is to superiors, to those whom God has specially appointed to instruct and guide others, that Jesus appears. We know not what passed between Jesus and Peter when he was favoured with this blessed apparition, and we may not ask or seek to know why our superiors give certain directions, or refuse certain permissions, or grant certain dispensations. It is enough for us that Jesus appears to Simon. We are not worthy to know what they know and see. We are not worthy to be enlightened as they were enlightened, and even if we were worthy, sweet Jesus teaches us through others, and through others only can we know His will in questions of obedience. And yet even for superiors the risen Heart of Jesus has an instruction. They may not despise the message "of the women"; they may learn in hidden ways from the feeblest and the poorest of their charge, and, like Peter, they also should rise up quickly, examine carefully, and consider prudently, if they hope, like him, to decide in truth on what may be a divine inspiration.

SECOND POINT –

Consider how we may glorify the Risen Heart of Jesus, appearing to Peter. Let it be by faithful and humble submission to our superiors, and by promptness in disclosing to them all that concerns our spiritual state, even as the women related the message of the angels to the apostles. This done, let us rest in peace. The Risen Heart of Jesus loves us far better and far more wisely than we can love ourselves, and we may well abandon ourselves utterly and unreservedly to His keeping.

ASPIRATION –

Risen Heart of my Jesus, enlighten and guide our Holy Father the Pope, and all superiors.

Form your resolution!

Easter Tuesday

The Risen Heart of Jesus, Appearing to Magdalen

"When he had risen, early on the first day of the week, he appeared first to Mary Magdalene, out of whom he had driven seven demons."

(Mark 16:9)

FIRST PRELUDE –

Consider the garden and the new tomb where Jesus had lain.

SECOND PRELUDE –

Pray that Jesus may visit you also at this blessed Paschal time, however sinful your past life may have been, and however unworthy it may have rendered you of such favours.

- Pause and Reflect -

FIRST POINT –

Who but Jesus would have appeared first to one out of whom He had cast seven devils? Courage, poor soul, overwhelmed with fear at the remembrance of past sins, and almost despairing at present imperfections! Oh, take heart! Jesus came to save. He came to seek out the souls who would not come to Him; He came to save the souls who seemed not to care for their salvation; He came to save the most worthless and wretched of His creatures; and yet we might well have supposed that after they had killed Him, after they had treated Him as an enemy, after they had done their worst to injure Him, that now, at least, He would deem something due to justice, and close the long-open account of mercy. But no, the Risen Heart of Jesus—blessed be His sweetest name—loves poor sinners as fondly, and tenderly, and unreservedly, as the Crucified Heart had loved them; and He appears first to Mary Magdalen, out of whom He had cast seven devils.

SECOND POINT –

Let us consider how many devils sweet Jesus has cast out of us. Alas! Have we allowed Him to cast out seven? Have we never invited them back after He has freed us of them? And if we are so happy as to have preserved our baptismal innocence, to have kept ourselves in all the purity of our first communion, or our solemn consecration to God, are we keeping those evil spirits not only out of our souls, but also at a distance from them? How often we permit them to linger near us, to walk round us, when by one heartfelt prayer, one earnest act of love, one fervent act of contrition, they might be driven from us, perhaps forever? Oh, let us endeavour, at this blessed Eastertide, to be faithful to our Risen Love. He will appear to us, He will console us, He will strengthen us by His spiritual visits, in the Sacrament of His Body and Blood, and the whispers of His grace: only let us drive far from our hearts those enemies whom He has conquered for us.

THIRD POINT –

Let us consider how we may glorify the risen Heart of Jesus, appearing to Magdalen. Let it be by imitating her fidelity. She remained by the tomb of Jesus weeping, when others returned to seek rest or consolation in their homes.

O true, loving-hearted one, O faithful Magdalen, obtain for me a rich share in your fidelity and your love. May I ever remain with you by the tomb of Jesus, finding more pleasure in His lonely sepulcher than amid crowds of friends or social joys. Some are willing to remain with Him, or some few blessed souls stay with Him on Calvary; but they are most blessed and most faithful who remain also by His tomb, grieving His absence, content to be without all consolation until His return—He Whose excessive love binds them to the very stone which hides Him from them, when He can no longer be found elsewhere.

ASPIRATION -

Risen Heart of Jesus, drive far from me all Your enemies.

Form your resolution!

Easter Wednesday

The Risen Heart of Jesus, Consoling Magdalen by a Vision of Angels

"But Mary stayed outside the tomb weeping. And as she wept, she bent over into the tomb and saw two angels in white..."

(John 20:11–12)

FIRST PRELUDE –

Consider the faithful Magdalen, weeping because she can no longer find Him who is her only joy.

SECOND PRELUDE –

Pray that henceforth you may only weep for and with Jesus, and that you may seek Him alone in all places and occupations.

- Pause and Reflect -

FIRST POINT –

The disciples go home when they find the sepulcher empty. Even faithful Peter and loving John are content with "looking in and seeing the linen clothes," but Magdalen remains, weeping. If she cannot see Jesus, she will at least remain where she knows He has been. Oh, how fondly earthly love treasures the relics of the departed, loves to stand where they have stood, to sit where they have sat, to keep what once was kept or cared for by them! And why may not the faithful Magdalen treasure as tenderly the grave cloths or the tomb of her only love! And those who stand weeping and watching for Jesus through the long night of life, shall surely find Him Whom they have wept and watched over, in the brightness of eternal day.

SECOND POINT –

Let us consider how we may imitate the example of Magdalen. Oh, let us stand weeping by the tabernacle, where Jesus truly lies hidden in the adorable Sacrament of the Altar. We may not feel conscious of His presence, we may not see Him, our night of weeping may be long, but the morning of joy shall surely come. Neither angels nor apostles could comfort Magdalen in the absence of her Lord. If we would imitate her, and share in her rewards, let us not seek comfort from any but Jesus. Let us prefer remaining near His sepulcher, weeping, rather than enjoying the gladdest of earthly delights apart from Him; and from time to time, as we make acts of humiliation and burning love, we shall see angels sitting, we shall receive holy inspirations, holy consolations, and glimpses of eternal joys.

THIRD POINT –

Let us consider how we may glorify the Risen Heart of Jesus, consoling Magdalen by a vision of angels. Perhaps we may do so most effectually by endeavouring to increase in fluent devotion to Jesus in the adorable Sacrament of the Altar. The angels are never absent for a moment from the tabernacle; their life is one perpetual act of adoration and praise. Let us try to imitate them, let us carry all our griefs, and trials, and anxieties to Jesus, and if duty calls us for a few moments to His presence, let our first thought be of Him. Let us seek to have some special intention each time we kneel before the altar, or on returning to or leaving the choir. Love is fertile with suggestions, and Jesus will Himself teach us how to adore Him best.

Aspiration -

Sweet Sacrament, I adore You, may I love You more and more.

Form your resolution!

Easter Thursday

The Heart of Jesus, Appearing to Mary Magdalen as the Gardener

"...she turned around and saw Jesus there, but did not know it was Jesus."

(John 20:14)

FIRST PRELUDE –

Consider Jesus appearing as the gardener.

SECOND PRELUDE –

Pray for the grace to seek Him in every place with the same love as Magdalen.

- Pause and Reflect -

FIRST POINT –

Magdalen had been conversing with angels, and they had inquired as to the cause of her grief; but as they had not told her where her Lord was, she turned back from them. Even angels cannot satisfy the soul which seeks the Lord of Angels. Even the purest, the holiest of spiritual joys, is not enough for the soul which pines for God alone. Oh, how happy and how blessed shall we be, if we thus seek our Lord. Oh, let us "turn back" from all that hinders or tempts us, however good it may appear, when we are seeking Jesus. Oh, let us never rest until we find Him. The joy of that finding will be proportioned to the earnestness and love with which we have been seeking.

Second Point –

"She knew not that it was Jesus." How often we know Him not, even when He is nearest to us. He speaks to us, but we do not recognize His voice; He appears to us, but we do not discern Him. We blame the unfortunate accident, the trying delay, the unkind action, the thoughtless word, the little neglect, the apparent or real slight, the want of consideration for our feelings; and we say, *if this had not happened—if that person had not been so neglectful—if those plans had not been crossed how much better it would have been*; and we know not that it is Jesus, sweet Jesus, the truest, tenderest, gentlest lover of our souls. He is standing by us, quite near, but we think it is the gardener; He is watching us closely, but we are too absorbed in our trial or vexation to notice Him; even when we are seeking Him, seeking earnestly and faithfully, we often know Him not when He is nearest to us, for the trial He has sent so absorbs us that we forget to recognize His hand in its every circumstance, and to believe in His love through all its pain. Oh, if we only knew that it was Jesus, how differently we should act in many circumstances, in every trial; and yet, are we not well aware that He who has numbered the hairs of our head watches over and appoints each, and even the most trivial, circumstances of our daily lives?

Third Point –

Let us see how we may glorify the Risen Heart of Jesus, appearing as the gardener. Let it be by confiding our souls entirely to His care. He is, indeed, the Gardener. Let us give Him full and unreserved charge of the mystical garden of our souls. Let us ask Him to plant, and to water, and to prune as He wills; let us offer Him our love and the fruits of our sacrifices. It is true He can take them if He chooses, but should we not love the merit of offering them to Him ourselves? Why should we deprive Him of the glory which we may give Him by the generous exercise of our own free will? When we are suffering, and dejected, and disappointed, let us say also: it is the Gardener. But let us remember who that Gardener is. In summer and winter, in heat and cold, early and late, He toils and labours, and He waters the plants He has set with blood. Oh! Shall we ever again distrust His love or doubt His care?

ASPIRATION -

Risen Heart of My Jesus, I give you the flowers of my love and the fruit of my sufferings.

Form your resolution!

Friday in Easter Week

The Heart of Jesus, Conversing with Magdalen

"Jesus said to her, 'Woman, why are you weeping? Whom are you looking for?'"

(John 20:15)

FIRST PRELUDE –

Consider the garden, and Jesus standing and addressing Magdalen.

SECOND PRELUDE –

Pray for the grace always to hear the voice of Jesus whenever, wherever, and however He may address you.

- Pause and Reflect -

FIRST POINT –

Jesus speaks to Magdalen, but although she seeks Him so earnestly, she discerns Him not. Is not this often the case with us? Unexpected trials come, we forget they are from God, and their suddenness takes us off our guard. We pray for some special grace, and God sends some special suffering: we do not see the answer to our prayers. Some affliction comes to us, apparently through our own fault, or through the fault of others: we do not see the hand of God. Oh, there is no peace like the peace of those who see God in everything, no love like the love of those who trust God in everything. Our Lord told Saint Gertrude that those who conquered nature should be as a pillow on which He would repose. Who would not desire to attain this honour—to receive this favor? O Christian soul, trust, trust, trust!

Second Point –

Consider the manner in which Jesus makes Himself known to the faithful soul. He has spoken to her, and she knows Him not. He says but one word, "Mary," and she falls at His blessed feet in an ecstasy of adoring love. He calls her by name, and by the name dearest to His risen Heart—"Mary." He will not add Magdalen, for Jesus seldom reproaches, and we know how He overwhelms the souls who seek Him faithfully and constantly, with the tenderest caresses and deepest love. "Mary!" The Heart of Jesus never changes. He loved the penitent one on earth, and He loves her still in heaven. O Jesus, sweet Jesus, when will You call us also by our names in heaven, as You have so often and so sweetly called us upon earth? "Mary!" O dearest Lord, say but that word again. The voices of angels have sounded in the ears of Magdalen, and their music might well soothe and banish every earthly care; but to her no voice but one could satisfy, and that Voice has spoken and called His sheep by name. O our Risen Love, call us also, for we have sought You, we have longed for You, we have wept for You. We also will say Rabboni. Whatever happens, it is the Master; whatever tries us, it is Rabboni's good pleasure; whatever gladdens us, it is an echo of Rabboni's voice; and so we also will answer at all times, in all places, under all circumstances, "Rabboni." Our utterance may be broken by tears, but it will not be the less loving, nor the less trustful. It may not be heard or known by mortals, but the listening ear of Jesus treasures our every accent, and He will reward a thousandfold our faith, and love, and trust.

Third Point –

Let us see how we can best adore our Risen Love, conversing with Magdalen. Perhaps we might do so in two ways. First, by an unbounded trust in our Master's love, whether He manifests Himself to us openly, or tries us in hidden ways; by saying *Rabboni* under every trial; by remembering that the Master is our Father, our Brother, and our Friend; by submitting lovingly to His will, however manifested to us. Secondly, by learning from the example of Jesus, the tenderest charity to others. It is no business of ours whether our neighbors' sufferings are sent in judgment or in mercy; let us only seek to soothe and console them in the kindest manner. Let us call them by the name they love best to hear; let us offer the consolations and attentions which will please them most; let us learn that thoughtful love which divines the wishes of others, and offers a kindness, not in the way most pleasing to ourselves, but in the way most pleasing to them.

Form your resolution!

Saturday in Easter Week

The Risen Heart of Jesus, Appearing to His Blessed Mother

"My lover belongs to me and I to him… Until the day grows cool and the shadows flee."
                              (Canticle 2:16, 17)

FIRST PRELUDE –

Consider the patient and ecstatic love with which Mary waits for the first apparition of Jesus.

SECOND PRELUDE –

Pray that her prayers may obtain for you the grace of a glorious resurrection, and of beholding the countenance of Jesus, gazing upon you with love and mercy.

- Pause and Reflect -

FIRST POINT –

The Virgin Mary had no need to watch over the sepulcher, for Jesus lay in her heart, in the adorable Sacrament of the Altar; according to a pious tradition, from the moment she received Him at the last supper until the hour of His resurrection. And even were it not so, her union with Him was inseparable—a union closer than the love of bride and bridegroom—a union incomparably beyond the closest union of the highest saint. The Flesh now glorified had been formed in her pure womb; the human life now exalted at the right hand of God had its first pulsations in her immaculate bosom; the Word which was made flesh and dwelt among us, first dwelt and was made flesh in Mary's womb. Oh, how glorious, how triumphant was His resurrection for her! Now her joys were consummated, and her sorrows consoled, in proportion to their greatness. The first public appearance of Jesus is to the forgiving and loving Magdalen, but the first secret embrace of His love was surely for His own faultless Mother.

Second Point –

Consider how Mary had longed for that apparition. She knew He would come. She had no doubt of the resurrection on the third day, but the shadows of Calvary lay dark and heavy upon her soul, until the dawn of that Easter morning. Her night had, indeed, been one of awful fear and untold agony. The demons of doubt and unbelief could not for a moment shake the firm confidence of her pure soul, but it may be they wreaked their vengeance on it all the more because of the very importance of their mightiest efforts. Perhaps nothing but the vision of Jesus Risen could have removed the painful image of her dead Son, which was imprinted on her heart. But the day breaks, and the shadows retire. The day of Mary's power commences, the day of grace, in which she enables us to rise victorious over sin and demons. Behold how she "comes forth as the morning rising, fair as the moon, bright as the sun, terrible as an army set in array": fair as the moon to console us, bright as the sun to fructify us, terrible as an army to defend us.

Third Point –

Let us consider how we may glorify the Risen Heart of Jesus, appearing to His blessed Mother. Oh, let us ask and pray that our Beloved may be "to us, and we to Him," until the day break, and the shadows retire, that we may seek nothing, desire nothing, look for nothing, but Jesus crucified, until the day of eternity breaks, when we shall share His resurrection glories in proportion to our fidelity to his cross and His sepulcher. The shadows of earthly grief, and care, and disappointment, will soon pass away; one glance of His love will turn them all into unchanging brightness and beauty. O Mary, by your joy in the resurrection of your sweetest Jesus, obtain for us the grace to ever live with eternity in view.

Aspiration -

My beloved to me, and I to Him, till the day break, and the shadows retire.

Form your resolution!

Ascension Day

The Heart of Jesus Glorified, Ascending to Heaven

"When he had said this, as they were looking on, he was lifted up, and a cloud took him from their sight."
(Acts 1:9)

FIRST PRELUDE –

Consider the Ascension of Jesus, and the looks of love and sorrow with which our Blessed Lady and the Apostles gaze upon our ascending Lord.

SECOND PRELUDE –

Pray for the grace to ascend to heaven in spirit today, and to learn thus to despise all earthly things.

- Pause and Reflect -

FIRST POINT –

Consider the glories and triumphs of our ascended Lord. Now, indeed, His sufferings are rewarded, and His humiliations are His eternal crown; and yet His ascension is only manifested to a few, for the great day of triumph is yet to come—the day of triumph and of fear, when all people shall behold His conquering majesty. It is so also with our Lord's most chosen servants. A few may witness, and almost envy, the happy death of some holy soul, who has been despised for renouncing the world, or embracing the true faith; but the vast multitude neither know of, nor care for, their blessedness. The poor man or woman, who has suffered long years of martyrdom of want and pain, dies also; and angels take the soul in triumphant jubilee to heaven; but the world goes on as it did on the day of our dear Lord's ascension, and misses the saintly and the poor as little as it missed Him. But the day will come when the world will be compelled to acknowledge them in shame and fear, and those dear souls shall receive a reward and a glory beyond their hopes.

Second Point –

"A cloud received him out of their sight." Even the Apostles were not privileged, while on earth, to see the triumph of their Master. The courts of heaven were ringing with alleluias as they had never rung before. The angels overflowed with gladness. The torrents of joy which ever pour forth on them from the bosom of the Eternal Father poured forth in new oceans of unbounded light and love. But even the Beloved Disciple, as far as we know, only saw the cloud which took Jesus out of his sight. And all that we can now see or know of heaven may be compared to this cloud. If we had even one glimpse of its brightness, perhaps we could no longer remain on earth. Happy for us if we raise no clouds of our own—no clouds of sin, or imperfections or coldness—to hide heaven even more from our gaze.

Third Point –

But there are some souls whom our Lord tries specially, by hiding heaven from them. They are sometimes the very last person to whom we should suppose He would send such a trial. There is not only a cloud, but a dark cloud before their eyes, when they try to gaze up after their ascending Lord. But heaven is not less bright because our eyes are clouded, either by our imperfections, or as a special trial of our love. Let us trust when we cannot see, and our trust will add to the very joys we find it so hard to realize. The disciples would rather have had the sensible presence of their Lord on earth, but He told them it was better for them that He should go to the Father. We would prefer consolations and spiritual satisfactions, yet is it not better for us also to have trials and desolations? But whether our path be in darkness or in light, let us join our voices with the angelic choirs today. Let us forget ourselves in Him. It is enough that He is glorified, that He rejoices, that He can suffer no more; and as we cannot open a window on the most burning summer day without feeling some little breath of air, so we cannot open the window of our hearts in generous thanksgiving, without receiving therein some little breeze of consolation, however dry and desolate our hearts may be.

Aspiration -

Ascending Heart of my Jesus, plead for me with the Father.

Form your resolution!

Pentecost Sunday

The Heart of Jesus, Sending us the Holy Spirit with His Sevenfold Gifts

*"Give me Wisdom, the consort at your throne,
and do not reject me from among your children...Indeed,
though one be perfect among mortals,
if Wisdom, who comes from you, be lacking,
that one will count for nothing."*

(Wisdom 9:4, 6)

"For the wisdom of this world is foolishness in the eyes of God..."

(1 Corinthians 3:19)

FIRST PRELUDE –

Consider the Eternal Wisdom, the Third Person of the Blessed Trinity, enthroned in heaven, where, from all eternity, He has dwelt; but from which He now descends, with the impetuous flight of love, upon Mary and the assembled disciples.

SECOND PRELUDE –

Pray that this Blessed Spirit may descend upon you today in all His fullness and in all His love.

- Pause and Reflect -

FIRST POINT –

   From all eternity, the Third Person of the Blessed Trinity had been enthroned with the Father and the Son. But He also would have His share in the salvation of the human race, that race which has loved so little. Jesus had promised us the Paraclete, and the Paraclete longed to come, not only because Jesus had promised His coming, but because He desired to come. What amounts of ingratitude, contempt, and indifference that blessed Spirit must have foreseen and accepted! From the world it might have been expected, but from the Church, at least, He might have hoped for love and thankfulness for His mission. But what practical recognition is there now of His office and His Presence? Where is the profound submission to His least whisper in the voice of the Church through which He speaks? Where is the constant, prayerful seeking for, and dependence upon His guidance, in the individual Christian?

SECOND POINT –

   Let us at least endeavour to meditate attentively during this week of graces upon the Holy Spirit's sevenfold gifts, that we may the better profit by them! And, first, let us meditate on the gift of wisdom. How high and noble it is! It sits on the throne of God. Oh, let us cry out with our whole heart today, "Give me wisdom, that sits on your throne." Sitting is a sign of judgment and authority; this is the office of the Holy Spirit, and by it He enables us to judge as God judges. It enthrones us, as it were, beside Him. We look down upon earth, and see as the angels in heaven. It teaches us what is truly wise and what is really foolish, and it enables us to act upon our knowledge. We may be very perfect "among the children of men"; our opinion may be sought and applauded, our wisdom commended; but if the wisdom of God is not with us, we shall "be nothing regarded." Consider how necessary, how essential it is to have this wisdom. How earnestly we should pray for it! The world has its own wisdom, but it is foolishness before God, and yet, do we not often prefer the world's folly to God's wisdom? True wisdom has only one end, and it sacrifices all for that end. The wisdom of the world has countless ends, and for these ends it demands many sacrifices.

Third Point –

The fruit of wisdom is peace. Peace is the beatitude of heavenly wisdom, and spiritual consolation is its special reward. If we have only one end in view, and if that end is God, we shall never be disturbed. Our peace will be continual and abiding. We shall leave the world to disquiet itself as it will about the follies which it counts as wisdom; we know of only one wisdom, and that is foolishness to the world. The world considers it the very consummation of wisdom to obtain riches, honours, and pleasures; we know that to despise them is the sublimest wisdom. Oh, consider how great a gift it is to judge all things as God judges, to estimate things as God estimates them, and to learn the majesty of this gift of wisdom. Consider how blessed it is to act as God would act, and then learn how holy is this wisdom. Consider what it is to be calm and unmoved in all adversity, and then learn what a treasure is this wisdom.

Aspiration -

Give me wisdom that sits on your throne.

Form your resolution!

Trinity Sunday

Glory be to the Father, and to the Son, and to the Holy Spirit.

FIRST PRELUDE –

Consider the Church: triumphant in heaven, suffering in purgatory, and militant upon earth; uniting in prostrate adoration before the throne of the ever-blessed Trinity.

SECOND PRELUDE –

Prostrate with the Church, and adore the Eternal Three.

- Pause and Reflect -

FIRST POINT –

What can we do today, but lie in prostrate adoration before the throne of God! We have meditated on the love of the Father, in the weeks preceding Advent; on the love of the Son, from Advent to Pentecost; and on the love of the Holy Spirit, during the blessed Octave which has just closed upon us. Now it only remains for us to anticipate our beatitude, to live in anticipation of our first day in heaven, and cry out with love, "O Blessed Trinity!" All day long the glorious chime is surging up into heaven; the angels hear the voices of men, and unite with them; the suffering souls in purgatory cannot think of pain—they cry also, "O Blessed Trinity!" and pine yet more deeply for the vision of God.

Second Point –

The weeks that follow Trinity Sunday seem like the weeks of eternity, if we could fancy the divisions of time to exist there. They pass on in calm, even measure. We honour the saints as their festivals come and go, or we praise the white-robed army of martyrs; but our hearts are not wrung as they are in Lent, when we think of the Passion; nor do weep as we must in Advent, because sweet Jesus is coming to suffer. Our occupation in these long weeks should be devotion and praise; not devotion of words, if that can be called devotion, but devotion of the acts of our whole lives and beings to the Blessed Three. Oh, if we could only fathom the depth of the meaning in that word "devotion"; if we could know the absolute, entire, unreserved sacrifice of self which it implies, and better still, if we could, in the strength of the Holy Spirit, commence now to practice it!

Third Point –

But this should be also a day of reparation—of reparations of praise to the Blessed Trinity for all the blasphemies, the indifferences, the insults of the creatures whom He has created, redeemed, and sanctified. Can we think of what men owe to God without feeling how deeply we are bound to reparations of praise? We must praise Him also for His own greatness and magnificence, rejoicing that He is what He is; and we must offer our lives to him as the best anthem of praise we can bring. Heaven will be eternal praise: perhaps earth would be more like heaven if we began the employment of thanksgiving here.

Aspiration -

Glory be to the Father, and to the Son, and to the Holy Spirit.

Form your resolution!

Some things to ponder:
I am quite taken by the Easter meditations of Margaret Anna Cusack because, while reading them, a central theme begins to emerge throughout the meditations, and that theme is love. Mother Cusack points out to us that the Resurrection is a manifestation of Jesus' love. She uses the term "Risen Love" several times in her meditations, reminding us of the profound love that Jesus has for us as His followers. She states that Jesus only asks for love, and that the Risen Heart of Jesus loves us far better and far more wisely than we love ourselves. This is Easter joy! This made the disciples run to the tomb to see what Christ promised would be the conquering of death, obtained through His love for us and through the Cross. This love is further expressed in the image of Mary Magdalen at the tomb, weeping over the loss of her Beloved. She seeks the Lord and discovers that He is truly risen as He has said, and she shares this good news with others. Mother Cusack urges us to go the same route as Magdalen—to seek the Lord, discover His Love, and share it with others. This love is further manifested for Mother Cusack at Pentecost, when the love of the Holy Spirit enkindles in the Apostles the gifts to bear fruit and share that love with others. The image of the Trinity is also an image of God's love, manifested to us in the persons of the Trinity, as Mother Cusack reminds us.

This image of love and the Resurrection reminds me of two great mystics in the Church: Julian of Norwich and Hadewijch of Brabant, both of whose writings I am sure Margaret Anna Cusack was familiar with. Love was the central theme for both Julian and Hadewijch; it was paramount in their experience of God. For Margaret Anna Cusack we can say the same, as this is expressed so clearly in her Easter meditations. Hadewijch once wrote: "What happens to me, whether I am wandering in the country or put in prison—however it turns out, it is the work of Love." Margaret Anna Cusack could say the same. From the founding of her religious congregation of women, to speaking out on behalf of the poor and on women's rights, to her many literary endeavors, and her persecution by certain members of the Church, love motivated her and gave her the courage to endure—because in the end, she knew the love of Christ that impels and endures. This Love is what was manifested at Easter, and it must be shared with all we encounter.

Ask yourself:
What does the phrase "Risen Love" mean to me?
How does the love of Christ impel me in my everyday living?
How do I share the good news of the Resurrection with others?
Go back to one of Mother Cusack's Easter meditations. Sit and ponder on the meditation, and allow it to help you experience Easter joy.

Let us pray:
O God, who gladden us year by year with the solemnity of the Lord's Resurrection, generously grant that, by celebrating these present festivities, we may merit through them to reach eternal joys. Through our Lord Jesus Christ, your Son, who lives and reigns with you in the unity of the Holy Spirit, one God, for ever and ever.
Amen.

(from the Roman Missal)

The Blessed Virgin Mary

Devotion to the Mother of God

Our Lady of Lourdes

Our Lady of Knock

Devotion to the Mother of God

Of all the magnificent works of God's creation, Mary, the Mother of Jesus, is the only absolutely perfect work. Now we know how men prize anything which they have made in proportion to its success, and in proportion to the time, labour, and care that it cost them. We see this in regard to works of art. How proud the inventor is when his long-cherished design is brought before the public and proves to be a success. It is his work, it is he who has planned, and devised, and designed, and accomplished this wonderful invention. It has succeeded. All his hours of weary trial are forgotten, all his cares and anxieties are as though they had not been. He beholds his labour complete and brought before the world perfect. He has succeeded, and we all know how the world honours success.

God is our Father, and we are His children. He has told us Himself that great as the love of an earthly father is for his offspring, it is as nothing compared with His love for us. All holy human affection is a little stream of charity flowing from the great eternal ocean of Divine Love. God is love, and all holy earthly love is a little drop of Divine Love distilled from that heart which is Love Itself.

When we have considered this subject well, we have at once the key-note to the honour of the Mother of God. Of all the millions of human beings whom God has created, she alone is perfect. We do not speak here of the adorable humanity of our Lord Jesus Christ, for though His nature, blessed be God, is the same as ours, yet it is also apart from ours. Mary, then, is the only human being who was created perfect and who remained perfect.

God, then, looks on the Blessed Virgin Mary with perfect satisfaction, because she is perfect. He rejoices in her, He is glorified in her, she gives Him more honour and glory than all His creatures. Can we not then understand very easily how it is that the Almighty Creator desires of all things to see this perfect being honoured by His creatures? Can we not easily see that those who love God will love Mary, and those who hate God will hate Mary? If we love a fellow creature, we love those who are dear to him for his sake, and we especially love those who give him honour. How much more should this be in things divine. Should we not love next to God the one who is dearest to God, and should we not honour after God the one whom He honours most, and who has given Him most honour?

Saint Francis of Assisi, Saint Bonaventure, Saint Alphonsus Liguori—all the ardent, fervent, seraphic lovers of Jesus Crucified—have surpassed themselves in their expressions of love and devotion to Mary, and in their acts of homage and reverence for her.

If Mary is sinless it is by the grace of God, as she herself proclaimed to the whole world in her great song of praise when she said: "My spirit rejoiced in God my Saviour." But Mary was perfectly faithful to the grace which God gave her, and this is where her glory and perfection lies. Even as we say, "It is God who has made us and not we ourselves," so does our Lady say that it is God who has saved her and not she herself. There are those who refuse to honour His most perfect work. We see, then, that it is our duty which we owe to God Himself, since one of our first duties as creatures is to glorify, and honour our Creator, and we do this when we praise and extol His glorious works, and especially the most glorious and the most perfect of all His works.

The greatest honour we can pay to any mortal is to trust him, to confide in him; and this is the special honour which the Church teaches us to pay to Mary. We are to honour her and confide in her as our mother. We need not say anything here of the love of mother and of child. All the world knows how close, how tender, how deep is this tie. The child is a part of the mother—the child is the offspring of the mother, and therefore it is that we find even in the most savage countries the love of mother and child to be as strong and tender as in more favoured realms. What will a mother not do or dare for her little one, and what will a son not do or dare for the honour of his mother?

And here is another reason why we should practice devotion to the Mother of God. She is the Mother of Jesus, and this at once places her in the most exalted position to which any creature can be elevated.

Already Mary has begun her mission of joy to the human race, already souls leap with joy at the sound of her voice; already miracles are worked by the very accents of her voice, already the pure and the saintly know her as the Mother of God. Let us then say, with heart and soul, as Saint Elizabeth said nearly two thousand years ago: "Blessed are you among women, and blessed is the fruit of your womb."

Some things to ponder:

In 1880, Margaret Anna Cusack published her book entitled "Life of the Blessed Virgin." This work was an enormous undertaking, in which she wrote in great length on the life of the Blessed Virgin, as prefigured in the Old Testament, apocryphal writings, stories from the New Testament, and stories taken from visions of Mary that were reported as taking place around the time that Margaret Anna was writing her book. Overall, the book gives the reader a clear understanding of devotion to Mary in the Church of the nineteenth century. Many of these writings would challenge Margaret Anna in later years after she left the Catholic Church and resumed her identity as a Protestant. Catholics and Protestants view Mary in different ways, and Margaret Anna would later return to the Protestant understanding of her. Nonetheless, what she wrote as the "Nun of Kenmare" is what she believed at the time she was writing. Margaret Anna outlines in a beautiful way who Mary is to the Church, how important she is in the life of a Catholic Christian. Since her writings on the subject of Mary are rather lengthy, I have chosen three meditations from Margaret Anna's book to give the reader a taste of how she treats the subject of Mary. These are not the meditations in their entirety, but are core excerpts from each meditation.

This first topic on which Margaret Anna reflects is devotion to the Mother of God. Her two main reasons for such devotion: First, Mary is the perfect creation of God; and second, Mary is the Mother of Jesus. These two reasons alone sum up for us why there should be devotion to Mary. When we honor Mary, we honor God. We give praise to God through Mary and through her example. Through Mary we learn what trust and confidence in God really is. Through Mary we are reminded that we are created in the image and likeness of God, and we must mirror that. Mary can teach this, according to the thoughts of Margaret Anna Cusack. The Blessed Mother is blessed among all women, and all generations will call her blessed.

Ask yourself:
How do I view Mary?
What devotions do I foster to show my love for Mary as the Mother of God?
In her meditation on Mary, the Mother of God, what images of Mary does Margaret Anna Cusack use to help us in our devotion to her?

Let us pray:
O God, who through the fruitful Virginity of the Blessed Mary bestowed on the human race the grace of eternal salvation, grant we pray, that we may experience the intercession of her, through whom we were found worthy to receive the author of life, our Lord Jesus Christ, your Son, who lives and reigns with you in the unity of the Holy Spirit, one God, forever and ever.
Amen.

(from the Roman Missal)

Our Lady of Lourdes

Of all the famous shrines and sanctuaries of the Mother of Jesus, Lourdes has been, and probably always will be, one of the most famous. The circumstances connected with the beginning of the devotion to this shrine are full of interest, and the facilities of transit from place to place at the present day have made them so well-known as to render a full account of the original story unnecessary. Still, a brief sketch of the apparitions of Our Lady of Lourdes may interest even those who are happily familiar with the details but who will not, therefore, be unwilling to have them repeated.

On the 11th of February, 1858, three poor little girls went out to gather sticks in the neighborhood of the town of Lourdes. This town is situated in France, in the Hautes-Pyrenees, and has about five thousand inhabitants. The children were Bernadette and Mary Soubirous, and Joan Abodie. Bernadette was fourteen years old; the other two were eleven and fifteen. Bernadette was always a delicate child, and the great poverty of her parents prevented them from having sufficient food; so great, indeed, was their need, that they could only obtain fuel by gathering sticks which there, happily, the poor were free to do. Bernadette had been employed, like so many little saints since the time of the shepherds who were present at Our Lord's Nativity, in keeping sheep.

On the 11th of February, 1858, she went, as we have said, to gather sticks with her little companions; but her mother made her wear stockings, which the other girls did not do; Bernadette was also made to wear her *capulet*, or little cloak, a garment which covers the head and falls nearly to the ground. The girls went down the meadows until they came opposite to some rocks called *Massabielle*, or the old ricks. They were about a mile out of the town of Lourdes. Here they saw plenty of firewood lying about the rocks, and as the little stream was almost dry, they prepared to pass over it and gather the wood. In front of the rocks there was a cave or grotto thirteen feet high and three times as wide, and above this grotto were two openings, one of which was an oval shape, and high enough for a person to stand upright in. This was eight feet above the ground. The rocks above towered to an immense height.

Bernadette was preparing to cross the stream, when she heard the loud noise of a rushing wind; and looking up at the grotto she saw, in the niche of the large cave, that vision of beauty which henceforth was never more to leave her heart. This vision of surpassing beauty was clothed in white, with a white veil on her head. A blue girdle was tied loosely round her waist and fell in two bands almost to her feet. Her feet were uncovered, but upon each was a golden rose. She wore no crown or jewels, but her hands were clasped; a rosary, the beads of which were white and crystal, and the wires gold, hung from her fingers. Her eyes were blue and her features of surpassing sweetness.

Bernadette fell on her knees, and looked again and again at this marvelous vision. The lady smiled at her but said nothing, and the dear, faithful child, true to the sublime instincts of sanctity, took out her rosary and tried to make the sign of the cross, but amazement paralyzed her. The lady then took up the gold cross of her rosary and made the sign of the cross with it in a singularly graceful manner, and made a sign to the child to do the same. Bernadette did so, and ever after, none could fail to remark on the rare grace with which she made this holy sign of the Catholic faith. Our blessed and most sweet Mother Mary then passed her beads through her fingers, as if to show the child that it would be pleasing to her to say these prayers, and the obedient child then said her rosary.

When Bernadette had finished her rosary on her poor, little, humble beads, Our Lady smiled at her and made a sign to her to approach, but Bernadette feared to come, and the vision passed away. Happy child! All the wisdom of all the wise ones in the world, and all the priests and doctors of the Church could have given her no better advice than that which her saintly instinct taught her: to say the rosary. If the vision was a delusion, she was going the safe way, to the protection of prayer. If the devil was trying to deceive her, he was driven away the moment she called on the all-powerful Mother of God. And if it was Mary! Mary her own Mother! What do mothers love so much as to hear their children call them by their name. Let us do so even now, and say—Hail, Mary! Hail, Mary!

Later, Bernadette would ask our Lady on several occasions to tell her who she was. During the middle of March she went several times to the grotto, but without seeing the apparition. On the 25th of March, so happily called Lady Day (The Feast of the Annunciation), the day on which our Queen was proclaimed, by the voice of the Angel Gabriel, to be the Mother of our King and only love, Jesus, Bernadette felt an interior call to the grotto. It was a call which she understood so well; that interior voice with which the Beloved speaks to his beloved even in the descent of time; that voice whose unutterable sweetness can only be known to those who have heard it; that voice which is understood more plainly than any human sound by those who are permitted to hear it.

When Bernadette entreated, for the fourth time, that the beautiful woman tell her who she was, Our Lady disjoined her hands, placing her rosary upon her right arm and then, as she loosed her hands and clapped them, as if with a fervor of thanksgiving, she looked up to heaven, and said: "I am the Immaculate Conception."

It was another magnificat before the whole world! "My spirit rejoices in God my Saviour. He that is mighty has done great things for me, holy is His name."

With her pure hands clasped in thanksgiving, with her eyes bright with the light of heaven, and looking up to her God, Mary tells her name: "I am the Immaculate Conception." This is her name of predestination, this is the name of her joy, this is the fountain of her love of God. "I am the Immaculate Conception." All the power which God has given her flows from this, and all the honour that God has given her, its source and consummation, is here, and all this vision of beauty at Lourdes is to tell the poor world the great truth. It is the key-note of the life of Mary, and the completion of her honour. The whole world is dead and dark because of the sin of Eve.

The vision at Lourdes was a public sign to the whole world that this definition of Mary's identity was the will of God. Every miracle that has been, and that will yet be worked there, sings as the sons of the morning sing: Mary is the Immaculate Conception.

Bernadette who, as we have already said, was quite uneducated, and who had spent all her time herding sheep in the country, had never heard the words "Immaculate Conception." But the true-hearted, faithful soul was wiser than the millions who had heard it. She received the heavenly message and cherished it with all her care and love. She went directly to the local priest's house, and all along the way she said to herself: *Immaculate Conception, Immaculate Conception*, lest she might forget these new and strange words. So will the angels sing, all the long day of eternity, their hymns of thanksgiving; for the praise of the Immaculate Conception never, never ceases, since Mary is the immaculate Mother of the ever living God; and it is for and because of the greatness of His Divine Majesty that His Mother is Immaculate, and free from every stain of sin.

Some things to ponder:
In her book *Life of the Blessed Virgin*, Margaret Anna Cusack writes about several shrines and apparitions of the Blessed Virgin Mary. In the previous mediation, she recounts the story of the apparitions at Lourdes. She begins by acknowledging that Lourdes is, and will always be, a sacred and miraculous place because of what happened there. What is amazing is that the apparitions took place only twenty-two years before Margaret Anna wrote her book. She lived during the time of the apparitions. Her account is so detailed that it seems as if she had been

an eyewitness, or as if she had interviewed Saint Bernadette herself. I am certain that Margaret Anna had direct knowledge of what she wrote about; she must have heard accounts from people who were eyewitnesses, and read what Saint Bernadette herself spoke of to the world.

In the previous pages, I selected portions of the original mediation which I felt best highlighted the key message, facts, and details of Lourdes as transcribed by Margaret Anna. She includes this apparition in her book on the life of the Blessed Virgin because she wants to verify the doctrine of the Immaculate Conception. The Lourdes apparition helps us to understand that Mary was born without original sin. As Margaret Anna states, this apparition was a public sign to the world that Mary is the Immaculate Conception, and it places her in a special category for us, as Christians, to honour her as the sinless Mother of God.

These apparitions helped to enhance Margaret Anna's love and devotion for Mary, strengthening her faith through this newly defined (at that time) Catholic doctrine.

Some questions to consider:
Why is Mary's Immaculate Conception so important to the Church? What does this doctrine do for our understanding of Jesus Christ? At the beginning of this meditation, Margaret Anna predicts that this devotion to Our Lady of Lourdes will always be beloved to Catholics; why do you think she said this?

Let us pray:
Grant us, O merciful God, protection in our weakness, that we, who keep the memorial of the Immaculate Mother of God, may, with the help of her intercession, rise up from our iniquities. Through our Lord Jesus Christ, your Son, who lives and reigns with you in the unity of the Holy Spirit, one God, for ever and ever.
Amen.

(from the Roman Missal)

Our Lady of Knock

Pride of life finds its place everywhere, and yet God gives examples enough of how He loves to honour the humble. At Lourdes the Mother of God came to a poor simple little girl, who knew little more than how to say her Hail Mary. In Ireland, our own Ireland, the Mother of God came to simple, humble men and women; to a despised people; to a cruelly persecuted race; and she came to us at a moment of our utmost need. On all sides we suffer, on all sides we are despised. What does this matter; if we suffer with Mary, we shall triumph with Mary. If we are despised with Mary we shall be honoured with Mary.

It is as if she would come to claim us as her own before the whole world, or as if she must show that we are indeed the children of her predestination and of her care. Our people are dying not, indeed, at once, but slowly, and none the less surely from the effects of famine. The world has little pity for us. Even those who should have been the first to come to our assistance have failed us; even too many of those of our own faith have been slow and cold in their efforts to help us. But what does it matter? We have Mary. The Mother of God does not despise us; the Mother of God is not ashamed of us. She comes to us with her hands uplifted in blessing, and consoles us with her presence and her love.

There may be a famine of earthly food in poor Ireland, but there is no famine of Faith. We are but treading the path of our fathers, who chose rather to suffer with God than to be honoured by the world without God. In the awful testing time of the "Reformation," we had our choice, and we chose God and suffering; Mary and poverty; Faith and reproach; and never, from that time to this, has faithful Ireland faltered for one single moment; although, again and again, she has been tortured and tried, and has blessed her persecutors, though she was never blessed by them. She has provided priests and bishops, nuns and religious orders for England; she has remained a living witness of truth to that nation; and now she offers the most glorious proofs of the Almighty Presence of God in His Church—miracles and miraculous lives—which ought to convince the most blinded that the finger of God is here.

The little village of Knock is situated about six miles from Clare Morris, in the County of Mayo, a humble church indeed to be the scene of such wonders. It is situated in the West of Ireland, where the famine has been most severe, and where the people have suffered so patiently, as, in truth, they have done in every part of Ireland.

The chapel is a small plain building, but as we give a correct engraving of it, there is no need for further description. We must add here, that even the special correspondents of Protestant papers have carefully examined the church, the schoolhouse, and the entire plot of ground, and have admitted, that however the extraordinary appearances have been effected, they could not have been caused by natural means, such as light thrown from a magic lantern. The place is indeed far too open on all sides to admit of any kind of deception or trickery. The chapel itself stands in an extensive yard bounded partly by a dilapidated wall about four feet high. Beyond this there is a large field and open country; a small schoolhouse stands inside the wall.

The first apparition was seen on the night or evening of the 21st of August, 1879, the eve of the octave of the Assumption. It was first seen by two women, both named Mary; and so little were they prepared to see anything supernatural, and so real did the vision appear, that both thought at first that they were looking at some statues which they supposed had been brought down from Dublin by the good priest of this church. However, these were not statues fashioned by human hands, but a vision from Heaven itself.

At first, Mary Byrne thought she was looking at statues which had been got for the church. But in a few moments, both men and women would be undeceived, and would know that God had granted them the amazing favour of being the first to behold this heavenly vision. Both women first saw the same vision, and both gave the same description of what they witnessed. Saint Joseph was at the end of the gable, near the West, and he appeared to incline towards our Blessed Lady, so that his profile was towards the awe-struck women. They remarked that so plain was the vision that he appeared aged, and the figure of Our Lady, as described by the women, is strikingly like the representation of the Mother of God as seen in the Catacombs, and as drawn by the early Christian artists. This we think is not a little noteworthy, as these good women could never have seen or heard of such representations. The next figure was Saint John. Some doubt has been expressed, or rather it has been suggested as possible, that this might have been Saint Patrick. While it is quite evident that some distinctive characteristic would have appeared, had it been the national apostle, we may also take it for granted that God would, by a special providence, have given those who first saw this vision the light to know what it meant. The devotion of the early Irish Church to Saint John is well known to those who have studied Irish annals, and in the beautiful language of a people at once spiritual and poetical, he was styled "John of the Bosom"— John who first lay upon that adorable Heart, and drank of its fountains of love and consolation.

But the greatest of marvels are the miraculous cures which are happening there day after day. In holy Ireland, where faith is strong and above all, where faith is free from the shackles and turmoil of worldliness, it is just what might be expected. The blind see, and the deaf hear, and the lame walk, and the world is taught that, wondrous as were the miracles of Lourdes, the miracles of Knock surpass them.

Oh! Be patient, faithful people of Erin—of the saints—be patient yet a little longer. If you have not the world on your side you have God; if you are despised by those who should be true to you, you have Mary.

Some things to ponder:

In her book *Life of the Blessed Virgin*, Margaret Anna Cusack devotes the last chapter to the apparition that occurred in her own beloved Ireland, the vision of which would come to be known as Our Lady of Knock. I have just provided some excerpts about the apparition from this lengthy chapter. While reading the chapter on Our Lady of Knock, it is clear how important and beloved this apparition is to Margaret Anna. She highlights what happened during the visions and reports the testimonies of villagers who witnessed the apparition, as well as provides ecclesiastical testimony to support the authenticity of the apparition. Margaret Anna also devotes a good portion of the chapter to the countless miracles that have occurred there since the apparition took place.

Margaret Anna Cusack's book, *The Life of the Blessed Virgin*, was written right around the time that the event at Knock took place, in 1879. It is interesting to read the testimonies of the villagers who witnessed the apparition; it brings it to life again, as if it were being seen at the very moment that Margaret Anna is recording it in her book.

So why is the apparition of Our Lady of Knock so important to Margaret Ann Cusack? I have come up with four reasons:

First, it is the only Church-approved apparition of the Virgin Mary in Ireland. Not only does Mary appear, but she is accompanied by Saint Joseph and Saint John the Apostle, as they gather around an altar with the Lamb of God. The vision was visible for several hours to the people who observed it. As Margaret Anna Cusack states in the opening chapter on Knock, Mary came to give comfort, courage, and support to the Irish people, who had been suffering for so many years. This apparition encouraged them in their faith.

The second reason this apparition must have been important to Margaret Anna Cusack is that she herself experienced a miracle in prayer when she visited the shrine. She suffered such poor health, along with mental anxiety and a bad heart condition; but she records that her health was restored during her visit to Knock, and this gave her the energy she needed to continue her work.

Third, Margaret Anna Cusack founded a Poor Clare Monastery at Knock. She reached out to the working girls in the area, and implemented educational programs for them. It was also at Knock that Margaret Anna met Honoria Gaffney, who would become Mother Evangelista, a co-founder of the Sisters of Saint Joseph of Peace. The Sisters of Saint Joseph of Peace germinated at Knock.

Finally, it was at Knock that Margaret Anna Cusack met with great hostility from politicians and church leaders, as she criticized them for not doing more to help the poor of Ireland. Her outspokenness was not well-received and even caused her to be met with death threats.

Margaret Anna Cusack experienced great encouragement and strength from the Virgin Mary at Knock, Ireland; it gave her the impetus to persevere in her work. We can ask ourselves this question: How does the apparition of Our Lady of Knock encourage us?

> Let us pray:
> *Our Lady of Knock, Queen of Ireland, you gave hope to your people in a time of distress, and comforted them in sorrow. You have inspired countless pilgrims to pray with confidence to your Divine Son, remembering His promise: "Ask and you shall receive, seek and you shall find." Help us to remember that we are all pilgrims on the road to heaven. Fill us with love and concern for our brothers and sisters in Christ. Comfort us when we are sick, lonely, or depressed. Teach us how to take part ever more reverently at Mass. Give us a greater love for Jesus in the Blessed Sacrament. Pray for us now, and at the hour of our death.*
> *Amen!*

Various Saints

Saint Joseph

Saint Francis of Assisi

Saint Clare of Assisi

Saint Joseph

Saint Joseph had precisely the two qualifications which made him the fitting spouse for Mary. He was of royal descent and thus the fulfillment of the prophecies was secured; he was of saintly life, or none other dared approach so near to the majesty of the Incarnate Word.

Oh, glorious Saint Joseph how shall we speak of you, and how shall we exalt you? As spouse of Mary you are admirable; as father of Jesus you are admirable; as the one man of all men chosen by the Everlasting God to guard the early life of the Infant Jesus, we know not how to praise you. It was the depth of your humility which brought down upon you such stupendous graces. Kings and emperors look for the most exalted, the most prudent persons, to have charge of the young princes of the royal house. The King of Kings looks into the records of the past, and into the records of the present, and into the records of the future; and His Divine Majesty finds but one Joseph. Oh prince of the princes of sanctity, Oh most royal of all the Kings of the earth; Joseph: brother, father, friend, protector, guardian of Mary and of Jesus—be our father and brother and protector, and friend also, for in our pilgrimage to the celestial city we need care like yours.

Oh, Joseph the carpenter, grand in your holiness, sublime in your humility, exalted in your virtue, tender in your compassion; look upon us, the exiled children of your spouse Mary, and help us to reach our home. If to you Jesus, the Incarnate God, confided Himself, what can we do better than consider ourselves to you also.

We pray you humbly, accept our confidence; take us into your keeping; let us visit Bethlehem and Nazareth with you, and in that supreme moment when the last sacraments of the Church are given to our trembling souls, then, just as you lay in the arms of Mary, breathing out your pure soul to God, be with us, and bring us safe to our Maker and our Judge.

In honoring Joseph, the Church has simply followed the Divine example. Strange is the evil mystery of heresy. What God honors it refuses to honor, and prides itself as wise when it is most truly foolish. Heresy follows the example of the Devil, its master, who hates most those who are most dear to God. The Church follows the example of her Master, and honors most those whom He has most revered. In the perilous times of later days the Church has shown a special wisdom in confiding herself to Saint Joseph. In all the perils of the Divine Infancy, Saint Joseph was the guide and director of the Lord of the Church. To this day, the Church has to contend with the wiles of the Egyptians and to cast down their idols. Who can so well assist her as that great saint who protected our Lord on His flight into Egypt? The Church has to teach the world, with its increasing luxuries of life, and its necessarily increasing indolence of spirit, that the Christian's life should be one of stern discipline and active effort. Is not the life of Saint Joseph a model of saintly labor and of contemplative piety? Holy Mother Church has to insist again and yet again, that the wisdom of the world is folly, and that the wisdom of God is the only wisdom.

To whom can she point the Christian soul so well as to Saint Joseph, the most exalted of all men who ever have lived, or ever will live? Yet he worked in the carpenter's shop at Nazareth, and asked for no earthly exaltment, waiting, like the patriarchs of old, for that which is eternal.

And if the Church needs, as in truth she does, a protector who shall have no ordinary power to help her, she finds one in Saint Joseph, the nearest of all mankind to God, in the honor conferred on him, the most powerful intercessor after Mary the Mother of God, in the Celestial Court.

To honor Saint Joseph, as he should be honored, needs no hyperbolic language, which is too often unwisely used, and an offence to those who do not understand the true grounds of Catholic devotion. The honor with which God has honored him is the source and ground of all the honor which has been paid to him by God's Holy Church, and no words can make that honor greater or more exalted in the eyes of men or angels.

Saint Francis of Assisi

First Meditation

Saint Francis is considered as an evangelical poor one.

First Prelude –

Consider Saint Francis of Assisi seated at table with his mother, Pica, and then rising quickly to give bread to the poor.

Second Prelude –

Pray for the grace to imitate this great saint in his love for the poor.

- Pause and Reflect -

First Point –

    Love of the poor is generally one of the first and surest marks of sanctity. Our Divine Lord has made it one of the special, if not the very special sign and pledge of love to Himself. Hence we find, in the lives of the saints, that their first impulse, after God has called them to follow Him in the highest paths of the spiritual life, is to give all to the poor. They wish to give all, because it is given to Jesus; and they could not be content with giving Him less than all. Let us ask ourselves if our love of the poor is anything like theirs. We can only measure it by our willingness to sacrifice ourselves for them.

SECOND POINT –

Generosity to the poor draws down upon the soul the most special graces, even when this generosity has not been practiced from very high motives. How great then will be the reward of those who practice it for God alone! Perhaps the first feeling of tender compassion which Francis felt for the poor was a little impulse of divine grace, the commencement of a full tide of grace. Had he not corresponded with this little impulse, perhaps the full tide would never have been poured forth on him. Let us learn, then, how important it is for us to follow the least good thought, to do the least good action. Let us examine ourselves, and see if we are prompt in obeying these inspirations. We do not know what we do when we resist the least inspiration. God will withdraw these special, precious little lights from us, if we are not faithful to them.

THIRD POINT –

"As long as you did it to one of these my least brethren, you did it to me." Consider the amazing love of our Dear Lord in saying these words: remember that He uttered them Himself. Oh, how happy shall we be, if we are privileged to do the least thing for His least brethren: for the little children, whom He loves so much; for the neglected, whom He always thinks of; and for those holy souls who consider themselves the least, but who shall one day rank among the greatest. O Saint Francis, our father, our dear father, pray for us. Obtain for us the grace, the honor, to do something, to do many things for the brethren of Jesus; obtain for us a share in your love of Him and of those whom He has loved so much.

Second Meditation

The Stigmata of Saint Francis

"From now on, let no one make troubles for me; for I bear the marks of Jesus on my body."

(Galatians 6:17)

First Prelude –

Consider the wild mountain of Alvernia, and Saint Francis praying there with his whole soul to God.

Second Prelude –

Pray for the grace of a similar fervor in prayer.

- Pause and Reflect -

First Point –

Consider what it is Saint Francis desires: he asks for suffering and for love. "O my Lord Jesus," he cries, "I ask of you to grant me two graces before I die: first, that I may feel in my body and in my soul, as far as possible, all that you endured in your bitter passion; second, that I may feel in my heart as much as possible of that process of love by which you were induced to suffer such torments for poor sinners."

He wishes to understand the greatness of the suffering, that he may fathom the depth of the love. Hitherto he has been an evangelical poor one, and a disinterested poor one; now he desires to become a crucified poor one. Life is drawing to a close, and suffering appears to him, after the experience of years, and on the verge of eternity, as the greatest favor which God can bestow. What a lesson for us of the value and efficiency of suffering, from the little pain of body or mind, which passes in a few moments, to the long hours, or months, or years, of mental or bodily anguish!

SECOND POINT –

Consider why Saint Francis desires suffering. Is it not that he may become like unto his Lord? Long years of seraphic communing with his God have not satisfied his blessed soul. He asks for more, he asks to bear the marks of the Lord Jesus. Not that he ever imagined or desired the favour which was to be conferred on him. Far from it, he desires ignominious suffering; he obtains honorable suffering. He desires to suffer with the King; he is privileged, as far as mortal can be, to suffer as the King. And we also, have we not asked to live a life of poverty, humiliation, and contempt? Have we not stretched out our hands and feet, that they may be nailed by the nails of our three blessed vows to the Cross of Jesus? And we also may dare to hope, that if we suffer with the King, we shall also reign with Him.

THIRD POINT –

Consider the result of this prayer: "Henceforth let no man trouble me." "Who," exclaims an inspired apostle, "who shall accuse against the elect of God?" Who shall condemn those whom He has justified? Who shall accuse those whom He has acquitted? If the marks of the Lord Jesus are upon us, none may dare to touch us. We are thereby sealed and set apart as His. There is no more "trouble" for the crucified soul; our "passion" has blunted the edge of all other pains. Henceforth the crucified soul knows only one suffering, and that suffering is her strength, her rest, and her joy. O Blessed father, O Saint Francis, obtain for us this grace, that we may be so "troubled" with the troubles of Jesus, and pierced with His grief, that no other troubles or grief may have power to move us.

Saint Clare of Assisi

First Meditation

In which Saint Clare is proposed as a model for fervor in obeying the call of God to embrace a religious life.

First Prelude –

Consider the young and beautiful virgin of Assisi, surrounded with all the world could give of wealth, distinction, and happiness; and consider her promptness in obeying the interior inspiration which she received to devote herself entirely to God, and the perfection with which she accomplished her sacrifice.

Second Prelude –

Pray for the grace to correspond as promptly with all divine inspirations.

- Pause and Reflect -

First Point –

Let us consider the promptness with which Saint Clare obeyed the interior inspiration to devote herself entirely to God. From her earliest childhood she had sought only to please Him more each day. Every little self-denial with which she was inspired by divine grace was promptly executed. There were no delays, no excuses. She deprived herself of food and of rest for the sake of Christ's poor, and later, under the magnificent apparel which her station in life compelled her to wear, we find that she mortified her body with hair-cloth. Each day's sacrifice, each day's correspondence with grace in matters which we too often think trifling, was preparing her for the crowning grace of her vocation. Had she not corresponded with these first graces, would she have received the last? Let us learn from our mother Saint Clare to obey divine inspirations with more fidelity and promptness; let us ask her to obtain for us this grace.

SECOND POINT –

Consider the perfection with which she accomplishes her sacrifices; consider her circumstances before she left the world; and then consider the circumstances in which she placed herself by taking this step. Rich, noble, surrounded with all that earth could give or heart desire, beloved by her family, loving them deeply in return; was ever domestic happiness more complete? Living a pious and devout life, practicing all the virtues of the cloister—such was the position of the noble Clare de Scifi. How many would have listened to the temptation to wait until they were older, to wait until this new order was better established. Surely she was pleasing to God as she was, as she benefitted others and edified all: what need, then, for this something more radical? Such is the reasoning too often urged on us by our artful foe, and how willingly do we listen to it!

THIRD POINT –

The saints are the stars of the celestial firmament, who light us on our way to glory; but if we do not avail ourselves of their example and intercession, how can we hope for all the graces we require in order to live as they have lived? Do we value the rich treasures we have in the saintly founders of our holy order? Are we as devout to them as we should be? Do we endeavor to imitate their example? Do we constantly ask their prayers? Today, at least, let us make many thanksgivings to our Heavenly Father, for all the graces He has bestowed on us. If we desire to be her true and faithful children, our Holy Mother Saint Clare will most assuredly help us, and who, except the sweet Mother of Jesus, would be so likely to intercede efficaciously? She has left us the tenderest, the most maternal of benedictions. She, at least, desired to show us she would never forget us, and shall we be neglectful or unmindful of her?

SECOND MEDITATION

In which Saint Clare is proposed as a model of devotion to the Most Holy Sacrament.

FIRST PRELUDE –

Behold Saint Clare, prostrate before the Blessed Sacrament, interceding for her native city.

SECOND PRELUDE –

Pray that, through her intercession, you may obtain a great devotion to Jesus in the Eucharist.

- Pause and Reflect -

FIRST POINT –

Let us consider the lively faith which our Saint Clare had in the Most Holy Sacrament. On two occasions we find her miraculously delivering the town of Assisi from savage enemies. And what is the means she uses? It is the exposition of the Blessed Sacrament. Always trusting with a childlike trust, always loving with a childlike love, we cannot wonder that her prayers already met with acceptance before the throne of God. In all trouble, in all necessities, Jesus was her refuge, and when did Jesus ever fail? The Moors trusted in their armies, the captains of the Emperor in their valour; Clare has only Jesus—Jesus hidden, silent, and apparently helpless in the tabernacle. But Clare knows that this silent, hidden, helpless Jesus, who seems to let us do what we like with Him, is still the God of Armies, the only sure refuge of the afflicted. Oh, that we had a faith like hers! Oh, that we, in all our necessities, fled to the tabernacle! Surely we should often have our prayers answered; surely our faith would thus become more lively.

SECOND POINT –

The most Holy Sacrament was also the source of all her sanctity, as well as the peculiar object of her devotion. Indeed, we may say that the Blessed Sacrament supported both her natural and supernatural life. We are told that her fasts were so continual as to have exceeded what nature could have borne, unless it was supported by some special grace. How, then, did she live? What sustained her in the pains of her sickness, the causes of her office, her long vigils, her ceaseless fasts? Truly it was Jesus. He was her daily bread, and her life was a life of ceaseless union with Him, by sacramental and spiritual communions. Behold her in the long silent nights, prostrate in the choir, when all have retired to rest. She cannot leave her Love, and in her sickness, He will not leave her.

THIRD POINT –

Let us seek to imitate this blessed saint, by uniting our exterior duties to an interior spirit of prayer and recollection. Above all, let us continually unite ourselves to Jesus in the tabernacle. Let us seek consolation, and help, and support from Him, and He will never disappoint us; and if we cannot beautify many altars, or furnish many churches with necessities for the divine service, let us, at least in spirit, make visits of reparation to neglected sanctuaries, and let us show by our manner, and still more in our hearts, the love we bear for Jesus, when in His presence.

Some things to ponder:
Throughout her writings, Margaret Anna Cusack reflects extensively on the lives of the saints. She wrote several books on Irish saints, especially Saint Patrick, Saint Brigid, and Saint Colomba. Her book on Saint Patrick was praised by Pope Pius IX. She was one of the first to write a biography in English on Saint Francis of Assisi. The previous selections are three saints very dear to Mother Cusack: Saint Joseph, after whom she would name her Sisters of Peace, and Saints Francis and Clare of Assisi, who, as founders of the Franciscan movement of spirituality, were influential in the spiritual life of Mother Cusack, who was a Poor Clare. The meditation on Saint Joseph was taken from her book *Life of the Blessed Virgin*. In this meditation she reflects on the important role Saint Joseph played in the life of the Blessed Virgin Mary. She highlights his virtues, calling all Christians to imitate them in their own lives. It was these virtues that were the foundation of the establishment of the Saint Joseph Sisters of Peace. One of her famous sayings about Saint Joseph was this: "Saint Joseph—it would seem as if peace was his peculiar grace." The gentle peacefulness of Saint Joseph gave the sisters an example to imitate.

The meditations on Saint Francis of Assisi and Saint Clare of Assisi are taken from her book *Meditations for Advent and Christmas*. Towards the end of this book, Mother Cusack provides several meditations on these founders for her Poor Clare novices. When writing about Saint Francis, she highlights his poverty and suffering as marks of holiness to inspire all Christians; while reflecting on Saint Clare, she emphasizes her prayerfulness, and especially her devotion to the Blessed Sacrament. In regards to these meditations, Mother Cusack wants the faithful to look such saints as examples and supporters in prayer, encouraging us to place our intercessory petitions before them. The question that she asks towards the end of her meditation on Saint Clare is a good one for us to think about as we honor the saints:

> The saints are stars of the celestial firmament, who light us on our way to glory; but if we do not avail ourselves of their example and intercession, how can we hope for all the graces we require in order to live as they have lived?

Let us pray:
Almighty ever-living God, by whose gift we venerate in one celebration the merits of all the Saints, bestow on us, we pray, through the prayers of so many intercessors, an abundance of the reconciliation with you for which we earnestly long. Through our Lord Jesus Christ your Son, who lives and reigns with you in the Unity of the Holy Spirit, one God, forever and ever.
Amen!

(from the Roman Missal)

Sayings of Margaret Anna Cusack to Reflect Upon

Poverty

Justice

Spiritual Matters

Poverty

"The knowledge of the fact of poverty in general: what is needed is to make that knowledge personal and practical."

"Jesus was quite too poor in the circumstances of His birth for the world to concern itself about Him."

"Every penny spent in the purchase of the Kenmare publications goes to charity. It goes to benefit trade in Ireland, and any profit that may occur is devoted entirely to the poor."

"The gospel has been preached long enough to the poor. Who will preach it now to the rich?"

"Consider Jesus lying in the manger as our great model of poverty of desire."

"I hope such a generous response may be given to my request, as shall induce me to continue my labours for my countrymen, and to refuse the large profit which might be obtained for the poor for other literary engagements of a less national character."

"If good Christians, who live in the world, shall have a munificent recompense for deeds of charity done to the poor for love of Jesus, how splendid will be the reward of those who have given up their whole lives to such actions!"

"...any wonder that the saints cried out for poverty, as people of the world cry out for riches? Is it any wonder that they became, as it were, beside themselves with a holy thirst for contempt? Is it any wonder if, like Saint Francis of Assisi, they make this poverty their master and their love, and ask for nothing but the straw of the stable, and the shelter of the barn, and the clothing of the poor?"

> "O sweet Francis! Evangelist of Poverty, pray for us, that we also, like you, may desire nothing but our most poor Jesus, and the wealth of His unquenchable love!"

"The first, the only visitors we hear of at the stable were poor uneducated shepherds."

> "He came in the silence of the night, in the darkness of the winter, in the poverty of a stable."

"Saint Patrick landed in Ireland in the early part of the fifth century. He was soon surrounded by ardent and devoted converts, whose one desire was to lead their fellow countrymen to the one Faith, and this being rapidly accomplished, each little colony of missionaries soon formed the nuclear of a religious establishment, where charity to the poor, devotional practices, and the increase of learning, were their daily occupation."

Some things to ponder:
The following are quotes of Margaret Anna Cusack taken from various books where she speaks out on the social issues of her day, namely the poor and poverty in general. As the Nun of Kenmare, Margaret Anna's life was steeped in the purpose of human rights. She spoke out and wrote extensively on this

topic. The plight of the poor was a popular topic for the Nun of Kenmare. As we reads and reflect on these quotes, we can see that her concern for human rights was rooted in her deep faith in God.

Her focus on poverty is one of action: the Christian is called to do something to help the poor and to draw attention to those in poverty. Margaret Anna often uses the story of Christ in the stable to emphasize that He came into this world poor, and identifies with the poor. Examples of those who have done something for the poor are seen in the lives of Saint Francis of Assisi and Saint Patrick of Ireland. They both identified with the poor, and reached out to help them.

We can ask ourselves: how do I identify with the poor? In what ways can I reach out to the poor in my local community? What gospel passages help me to be more conscious of the poor?

> Let us pray:
> *Almighty and most merciful God, we remember before you all poor and neglected persons whom it would be easy for us to forget: The homeless and the destitute, the old and the sick, and all who have none to care for them. Help us to heal those who are broken in body or spirit, and to turn their sorrow into joy. Grant this, Father, for the love of your Son, who for our sake became poor, Jesus Christ Our Lord.*
> (from the Book of Common Prayer)

Justice

"There are few who do not admit that the poor need justice to be done to them, but the manner of doing the justice is quite another question."

> "Sooner or later, even in this world, every outrage against justice is punished, because an outrage against justice is an outrage against God."

"But, we are told now, even by those who are anxious to do some little act of justice to Ireland, that we must have coercion first, and justice after."

> "The Irish are eminently a justice-loving people. Let justice alone be granted to them, and there is that in their national character which will make them accept as a boon what others might accept as a right."

"But ours is, in many respects, an age of historical justice, and truth will triumph in the end."

> "The Lord to Saint Gertrude: 'Whenever the love of justice or of souls shall prompt you so to speak, my clemency will previously admonish the sinner you thus address to repent of their sins, so that they may not deserve vengeance or punishment by making light of your instructions.'"

"History repeats itself. It may be useful to remember this at a time when there is a probability of another revolution, none the less dangerous to public safety because it has its inception in a demand for personal liberty—not indeed the personal liberty of individual freedom to justice, but the liberty to prevent the doing of justice by others."

"What misery has been seen—what has been committed, even in our time, by unjust pressure on the poor."

"But victory is not always on the side of justice."

"But justice was ever tempered by mercy, even when the spirit of the times required that stern judgments should be passed on those who rejected the message of peace."

Some things to ponder:
Margaret Anna Cusack lived in Ireland during the nineteenth century, and witnessed the Great Potato Famine which caused the loss of many lives, as well as the exodus of the Irish people to other shores. In England it was the Victorian Era: some in society experienced decadence, but the lives of many others were ruled by poverty. It was the rise of the Industrial Revolution that created unhealthy conditions in the factories and unjust wages for the worker. Charles Dickens' book *Oliver Twist* was one of the works of literature that exposed the horrors of the poor; such vivid images and their reality impelled Margaret Anna Cusack to spoke out against the injustices of her time. Social justice was as hot a topic for the Victorian period as it is for our own day and age.

Margaret Anna Cusack used her pen to fight for justice. She spoke out for the poor, women's rights, worker's rights, and just wages. This brought her into the arena with politicians and church leaders, and as has been stated before, this got her into trouble and gained her a bad reputation. But what Margaret Anna learned is that this is the price one has to pay when speaking out against injustice. In the gospels Jesus says: "Do you think that I have come to bring peace? No, I have come to cast fire upon the earth. And what will I but that it be kindled!" Jesus knew that not everyone would accept His message of love and peace, but that it would cause division; yet this should not stop the Christian from speaking out. This is what Margaret Anna Cusack did during her lifetime. The quotes in this section reflect her concern in this area of justice. If she were alive today I am sure she would be speaking out on justice issues that we face in society: war and peace, equality for women and all races, global warming, immigration, and of course poverty.

As we prayerfully reflect on these sayings of Margaret Anna Cusack concerning social justice, what issues are near and dear to our hearts? How can we speak out for the injustices of today and be a positive force in our current world?

Let us pray:
Grant, O God, that your holy and life-giving spirit may so move every human heart, that barriers which divide us may crumble, suspicions disappear, and hatreds cease, that our divisions be healed, we may live in justice and peace, through Jesus Christ Our Lord.
Amen.

(from the Book of Common Prayer)

Spiritual Matters

"I think our dear angels often visit us, and we are not aware of it."

"Consider how completely disinterested was the sacrifice of Saint Francis…He had one motive so sublime that every other motive would have seemed as nothing in comparison. His motive was Love!"

"Some are attracted to do good by active works of mercy and others are attracted to do good by a life of prayer and contemplation."

"The saints are the start of the celestial firmament who light us on our way."

"If you see a bad example, instead of it making you do wrong, it should certainly make you twice as perfect."

"What is it to you or to me what others say or do, except insofar as we are bound by our office to the care of the souls of others?"

"Happily, the good also have their desires, their object is good, or in simple words, their object is God."

"We have to live our life to know it."

"Act together in everything and you will be holy and happy children of peace."

"They who possess God possess all things."

"Be honest, see things as they are."

"Keep courage and keep cool."

"Material progress is too often a sign of spiritual decay, and it is all the more dangerous because the danger is hidden and blinds by its very nature."

"We may never meet in this world but I trust we shall spend a long and glorious eternity together."

"May Christ give us his holy grace, that no word of ours may ever hurt or harm his little ones."

"We hope that Catholic women will take up with new ardor the great work that lies before them."

"Charity
　in speech,
　　Charity
　　in action,
　　Charity
　　　in thought."

"To touch a soul, a soul must know and feel that you touch it."

"If the world is to be converted, and souls are to be won, and if God's Kingdom is to be advanced, it will be by deeds and not by words…"

"The highest duty of the creature is to praise the Creator, and service is the highest praise."

> "So long as your Christianity is merely theoretical, they are very well pleased with you, but once they find you are practical in carrying it out, they part company with you, angrily or scornfully…"

"Love contains in itself the perfection of faith."

Some things to ponder:

Spiritual matters encompass all areas of life. Not only was Margaret Anna Cusack a social activist who spoke out for the poor and the less fortunate: she was also a "Spiritual Mother." She had great insight into the spiritual life and she shared that insight with her religious sisters, first as a Poor Clare in Charge of the novices, and later as the foundress of the Sisters of Saint. Joseph of Peace. Her words of wisdom attracted many followers who sought her advice.

The greater part of this book contains her writings and meditations on the liturgical year. These meditations give keen insight into the depth of the spiritual life that Margaret Anna Cusack possessed. Another famous book of hers entitled *A Nun's Advice to Her Girls* was written to impart her spiritual advice to the girls entrusted to the care of the Poor Clare Nuns in Ireland. It was a way of helping the young girls of Ireland to grow and recognize their spiritual worth.

Take a few moments to read over Mother Cusack's sayings on spiritual matters. Choose two or three of her quotes to meditate on. What attracts you to these particular sayings? What advice is the Nun of Kenmare giving you at this moment in your spiritual life? How does the Nun of Kenmare challenge you right now?

Let us pray:

Direct us, O Lord, in all our doings with your most gracious favor, and further us with your continual help, that in all our works begun, continued, and ended in you, we may glorify your holy name, and finally, by your mercy, obtain everlasting life, through Jesus Christ Our Lord. Amen.

(from the Book of Common Prayer)

Sources

Constitutions of the Sisters of St. Joseph of Peace. Washington D.C. Sisters of St. Joseph of Peace. 1994.

Cusack, M.F. *The Life of the Blessed Virgin Mary, Mother of God.* London: Burns & Oates, 17 Portman Street. 1880.

_____. *Margaret Anna Cusack on Justice.* Baltimore: Peace works. 2003.

_____. *Margaret Anna Cusack on Poverty.* Baltimore: Peace works. 2202.

_____. *Meditations for Advent and Easter.* London: Burns & Oates, 17 Portman Street. 1880.

_____. *Meditations on the Passion In Honor of the Heart of Jesus Crucified, For Lent, or the Fridays Throughout the Year.* London: Thomas Richardson and Son. 1880.

_____. *The Nun of Kenmare: An Autobiography.* Boston, Ticknor and Company, 211 Tremont Street. 1889.

_____. *The Story of My Life.* London: Hodder and Stoughton, 27 Paternoster Row. 1893.

McClory, Robert. *Faithful Dissenters: Stories of Men and Women Who Loved and Changed the Church.* MaryKnoll, New York: Orbis Books. 2000.

The New American Bible. Wichita, Kansas: Fireside Bible Publishers. 2000-2001.

The Roman Missal. Washington D.C. United States Conference of Catholic Bishops. 2011.

Vidulich, Dorothy A. *Peace Pays A Price: A Study of Margaret Anna Cusack, The Nun of Kenmare.* Washington D.C. Sisters of St. Joseph of Peace. 1990.

Acknowledgments

I want to personally extend a "thank you" to Sr. Ann Taylor, CSJP (former provincial of the Sisters of St. Joseph of Peace, and now archivist) for her assistance and support to me during this project. She was so helpful in providing me with the resources necessary to make this book come about. She also opened the archives to me and lent anything I needed to help write the book.

I am also grateful to Msgr. Gerard McCarren of Immaculate Conception Seminary at Seton Hall University in South Orange, New Jersey. I am equally grateful to Mrs. Kim Cherevas, a parishioner from St. Mary's, Dumont, New Jersey, where I served as pastor. Both of these individuals proofread my work and made suggestions, and I thank them.

I also wish to thank Bishop John W. Flesey, Auxiliary Bishop of the Archdiocese of Newark, New Jersey, who provided the Foreword for the book and also read and made suggestions for the manuscript. I would also like to express my gratitude toward all of the Sisters of St. Joseph of Peace, Englewood, New Jersey, for continuing the vision of Margaret Anna Cusack, for being faithful women of the Catholic Church, and for encouraging everyone to stand for peace and justice.

I further extend my thanks to everyone at Leonine Publishers, who made the publishing of this book a reality. The publishing company is named after Pope Leo XIII, the great champion of Social Justice. This is ironic since he met and encouraged

Margaret Anna Cusack in her work and gave her permission to found her religious order. It is then only appropriate to publish this work here. Finally a specially thank you, as always, to my parents: Dom and Judy Ciriaco, and my brother Gerald for their love and support with any work that I do.

May God be praised!!

About the Author

Fr. Dominic Ciriaco is a priest of the Archdiocese of Newark, New Jersey, and a Candidate with the Society of St. Sulpice (Sulpicians). He was ordained in 1999 and has served as a parochial vicar, high school chaplain, and teacher as well as pastor. He currently is a member of the formation faculty of Theological College at Catholic University of America in Washington, D.C., which is conducted by the Sulpicians.

A Woman For All Seasons is Fr. Ciriaco's second book. His first book, *Witnesses to the Gospel: Reflections on Saints and Others Who Inspire*, was published in 2007.

 **About Leonine Publishers**

Leonine Publishers LLC makes fine Catholic literature available to Catholics throughout the English-speaking world. Leonine Publishers offers an innovative "hybrid" approach to book publication that helps authors as well as readers. Please visit our web site at www.leoninepublishers.com to learn more about us. Browse our online bookstore to find more solid Catholic titles to uplift, challenge, and inspire.

Our patron and namesake is Pope Leo XIII, a prudent, yet uncompromising pope during the stormy years at the close of the 19th century. Please join us as we ask his intercession for our family of readers and authors.

Do you have a book inside you? Visit our web site today. Leonine Publishers accepts manuscripts from Catholic authors like you. If your book is selected for publication, you will have an active part in the production process. This book is an example of our growing selection of literature for the busy Catholic reader of the 21st century.

www.leoninepublishers.com

www.ingramcontent.com/pod-product-compliance
Lightning Source LLC
Chambersburg PA
CBHW070638050426
42451CB00008B/213